CALLED BY NAME

Peter G. van Breemen, S.J.

DIMENSION BOOKS
Denville, New Jersey

Imprimi Potest: Eamon G. Taylor, S.J.
Provincial of the New York Province
August 22, 1975

*Dedicated to the Community of the Jesuit Novitiate
in Brussels, Belgium.*

Excerpts from *The Jerusalem Bible*, copyright © 1966 by
Darton, Longman & Todd, Ltd. and Doubleday & Company, Inc.
Used by permission of the publishers.

TABLE OF CONTENTS

FOREWORD

God called me by my name — that is my vocation. But it is more. It is my existence. When my parents had picked my name, plus an alternate name just in case, He had already called me by my name — that is why my Mother and Father expected me. My name enables me to be addressed and to respond, so that I can bear responsibility and fulfill a mission — it constitutes my identity.

This book offers some reflections on the God who called me into existence, into faith in Jesus Christ and into religious life. To the many persons who were instruments in the various stages of this call I am deeply grateful. It is through them that God's voice reached me and that I am who I am. I want to express particular gratitude to Sr. Theresa C. Falls, O.S.U., who was a faithful and tireless help in the writing of this book. She was so much attuned to its message that it could take shape through her. It was an inspiring privilege to work with her.

ONE

FATHER OF BELIEF

It is a commonplace of the Judaeo-Christian tradition that Abraham is "The Father of all believers" (see Rom 4:11). Soren Kierkegaard goes even further and calls him "The Father of belief." There at the beginning he stands—great, alone; yet his progeny extends incredibly, and we recognize that we too are related to him. In God's eyes he is truly our father in faith (Rom 4:17). This consideration, however, is meant to be more than a pious platitude giving antiquity and a certain respectability to our religion. A father is one who transmits life. Let us go, therefore, to this man who stands at the origin of our life of faith and pray that our own faith may grow and deepen. At a recent ordination ceremony in Holland there was inserted at the beginning of the long Litany of Saints the apt petition, "Holy Abraham, pray for us." Indeed, we can pray to him. Let us ask also that like him we too may become a father in faith, passing on to others this precious gift.

Abraham is first presented to us in the simple, direct call of God:

> Yahweh said to Abram, 'Leave your country, your family and your father's house, for the land I will show you. I will make you a great nation; I will bless you and make your name so famous that it will be used as a blessing.

7

CALLED BY NAME

I will bless those who bless you;
I will curse those who slight you.
All the tribes of the earth
Shall bless themselves by you' (Gen 12:1-4).

Until this moment scripture knows nothing about Abraham. It is only when he is addressed by God that he enters into history, which, therefore, is at the same time the history of salvation. Our first impulse may be to ask: "How does Abraham know that this voice is God's?" The question seems sensible enough; yet it is the wrong question, for there are three presuppositions behind it which make no sense. "How does he know that this voice is God's?" presupposes that we know who God is; next, that we hear in a human event a call; finally, that we conclude that these two go together, that the appeal comes from the God whom we know. But Abraham's call cannot be traced back to a god he knew. The decisive element in his faith is precisely that he did not know who God was; he had to leave behind all those notions and concepts of the divine he had hitherto held.

Like everyone else in his tribe and country Abraham had had many religious convictions. Even an atheist has them, for not to believe in God is in itself a religious conviction. What happened to Abraham was that he was summoned from these religious convictions to faith—a giant step. What he does is not to identify or to name the appeal as coming from God, but to respond to the call and to attribute to that summons such importance that all his previous concepts of god fade away. His experience of this God who calls, giving such promises, determines from now on what he believes about God. All that he had previously believed of the divine, all his prior religious convictions,

8

will henceforth be discerned as valuable only as they accord with this call.

Faith can exist only as a response to a call or to a revelation. If we want to know what it really is in the full sense of the word, we must go to that event where for the first time true faith occurred, i.e., with Abraham. Whenever we encounter faith, it is always in connection with this first moment of believing. And since its origin here with Abraham, faith has never ceased to be. The continuity of faith, the tradition throughout the generations is an essential element of faith. In his call and in his response to that call Abraham learns by experience the greatness and reliability of God. His knowledge of God is not the basis of his faith; it is, conversely, its fruit. And as it was with Abraham, so it is with us: faith is a continuous growing in that history we experience with God. Gradually for each one of us that perplexing, capricious little word *god* is transmuted into a name meaningful for us, but the transformation is achieved only on a long and arduous journey. At the outset, the word *god* is simply three letters, having reference to that which is unknown, possibly unknowable, and there stretches before us a long search during which this elusive concept develops from a meaningless cliché to the God who has called us by name and made us a people for himself. That long journey is the growth of faith, the evolution of prayer. Abraham's progress in faith was wholly characteristic. God called, Abraham answered, and in his response he grew in his ever-deepening knowledge of God.

The content of God's appeal was demanding: "Leave your country, your family, your father's house, for the land that I will show you." He has to leave. The security of the world familiar to him was to be left behind. For a

9

nomad that means much more than it does to us because nomads are more vulnerable; they need each other for mutual protection against the hardships of nature. Moreover, this call is imposed on Abraham without any explanation. God calls this hitherto unknown man from the security of his possessions and his country into the unknown, and this man hears that call and responds—that is faith for the very first time.

Abraham obeys that call. For the time being that is enough. Had he insisted on knowing more before he ventured his risk, he would have been showing the opposite of faith, which is never based on merely human assurance. Zechariah, who wanted to be sure, would insist upon some guarantees before yielding to God's word; that is not faith. Abraham, without knowing where he was going, went; that is faith. For each of us faith often implies that we too must set out:

> Listen, daughter, pay careful attention:
> forget your nation and your ancestral home,
> then the king will fall in love with your beauty.
> He is your master now, bow down to him (Ps 45:10-11).

The Little Brothers and Little Sisters of Jesus have a psalm on the call of Abraham:

> To leave Ur of the Chaldeans,
> to leave everyone and everything;
> to give up everything;
> to go away with nothing.
> Just to break all ties and bonds;
> to go away with nothing.

10

To leave Ur of the Chaldeans,
to leave on God's command.
The voice of God says "Go,
give up everything and go;
leave Ur of the Chaldeans,
into the desert, into the night!"

To leave Ur of the Chaldeans
with only God as pledge,
into the country of all joy
and all abundance,
into an innumerable offspring,
numberless as the sands on the seashore,
numerous as the stars in the sky,
to leave on God's command,
to leave Ur of the Chaldeans.

The initiative is God's. It is he who calls, and the person of faith responds. This receptivity to the appeal of God and the faithful response to it are still the core of all faith, for belief is possible only in the measure of our willingness to listen and to respond. That is why faith is always susceptible of growth. If we wish to renew our faith, there must always be a deepening of our eagerness to hear and to answer.

Then Yahweh promised: "I will make you a great nation; I will bless you." It is a mistake to fear that in the response to God there is a constricting of our lives, for the contrary is true: when we let God be God in us, we are neither shriveled nor stifled. By his very nature God cannot oppress; he liberates, as the psalmist recognized when he sang: "God, guardian of my rights. . .when I am in trouble, you come to my relief" (Ps 4:1). God wants us to unfold, and it is only when we repulse him, closing our

11

ear to his voice that we find a narrow-mindedness and a shallowness coming into our life. The certainty that God wants us to live, to grow and unfold, is basic to all authentic faith. Unhappily there are too many who consider God a threat, who are afraid to pray, for example, the prayer of abandonment of Charles DeFoucauld: "Do with me whatever you want," because they fear that having made this total surrender, they will find God jeopardizing their well-being by stripping them of what they hold dear. To think thus is to distort completely who God is and what his relations are with men. God is our creator, the one who has given us life in the first place, whose one desire for us is that this life may grow and increase to the full. By freely opening ourselves to the activity of God we are, as it were, letting him continue his work of creating, of bestowing life, so that we are more completely man in proportion to our receptivity for God.

Abraham's response to the call of God made him the father of many nations and gave world-wide, almost cosmic dimension to his fruitfulness. Possibly this is the criterion by which we can discern whether a call is from God or not. The call of God will always make us more ourselves, intensifying in us that fruitfulness which St. Paul calls the fruits of the Spirit: love, joy, peace, patience, gentleness, recollectedness (see Gal 5:22). It is senseless for a Christian to question whether he has the fruits of the Spirit. The right question is "Are the fruits of the Spirit growing, becoming more effective in me?" In fact, the sign that I am truly following the path along which God leads will be a genuine growth in these fruits. And conversely, if there is a decrease, I can question seriously whether I am on the right path or, even though I may be on the right road, whether I am proceeding at the speed God wants of me. Sometimes I may be going in the right direction but at too headlong a pace. The result will be strain, tension, a diminution of the fruits of the Spirit. On the other hand, if I progress too slowly on the right path, I shall find myself procrastinating and falling into a spiritual sloth that avoids necessary effort and makes growth in the spiritual life impossible. The increase of the fruits of the Spirit, therefore, is the ultimate sign of all discernment of spirits and is a positive indication that we are making the right efforts to respond to the call of God.

We may not yet realize the immense forces that are unleashed when our faith is carefully nurtured and fostered. Under its influence we shall be enabled to avoid the debilitating effects of mediocrity and to achieve that energetic thrust forward which will assure the spiritual growth that makes life worth-while. With God there are no half-way measures; his concern is not only that we may have life, but that we may have it to the full (Jn 10:10). We are faced constantly, therefore, with the need to intensify our faith, to deepen the generosity and the fervor with which we respond to God's call. And in all this there is an inherent apostolic dimension, for my own faith is the only ultimate support with which I can help others to believe. It may well be that this development of true faith in the man of today receives less support from social and ecclesiastical structures than in the past. As a result, we may feel a certain estrangement and a lack of affirmation by others. At such times, it may help us to recall Abraham, who in his days really was alone, the only man in the whole wide world who believed. He had no external support whatever, nor did he find any confirmation of that which he was accepting. So let us not complain! The conviction that not only our own personal good, but also the well-being of others really depends upon our faith can stimulate a certain generosity and impulse to action. At the moment when John Kennedy was summoning Americans to a new confidence in the tasks to be accomplished, he urged them not to ask what their country could do for them, but rather to ask what they could do for the country. That too must be our question: Not what support the community can give us in matters of faith, but what support and encouragement we can give the community. The service of helping each other to believe may be the best and most authentic service we can render. It is not easy to believe. If we can help each other in this, we shall have accomplished much for the well-being of all. Helder Camara, the bishop of Recife, has said that today, as yesterday, as always, mankind is carried and supported by "Abrahamic minorities," who have the courage to hope against all hope.

It is interesting to trace the growth of faith in Abraham and to watch its impact in his life. At first he responded to God's summons. Gradually, however, we see how his understanding of God and his realization of God's values shaped his life. Chapter 18 of Genesis gives us the beautiful story of his insistence in the face of an impending evil. We see Abraham "standing before Yahweh," pleading for Sodom, winning from God the assurance that the city will by spared if Yahweh finds fifty just men there, then forty-five, and so on down to the final promise: "I will not destroy it for the sake of the ten." Voltaire ridicules this passage, saying that Abraham here acts like a bartering, huckstering Jew. It is true that Abraham prays like a Jew, but whether we should mock him for this is another question. Prayer is the personal response of faith, and we must let each person pray in his own way. Since Abraham has been transformed into a believer, he has grown in concern for the people around

14

him, his companions in the city where they dwelt. His prayer shows a trust which we may call bold until we remember Christ's parables of the importunate friend whose midnight knocking was finally rewarded with the bread he needed. The lesson of Yahweh to Abraham is one with the lesson of Christ to his followers: perseverance is at once a condition and a sign of growth in faith.

But now comes the crisis in faith, the incident in which Abraham is to be tested in a crucible that tries him inexorably: "It happened some time later that God put Abraham to the test" (Gen 22:1-19). In one way or another faith must always face a test. The words of encouragement offered by Judith in a moment of great trial for the Israelites show how well the Jews had learned this lesson:

> Let us give thanks to the Lord our God who, as he tested our ancestors, is now testing us. Remember how he treated Abraham, all the ordeals of Isaac, all that happened to Jacob in Syrian Mesopotamia while he kept the sheep of Laban, his mother's brother. For as these ordeals were intended by him to search their hearts, so now this is not vengeance God exacts against us, but a warning inflicted by the Lord on those who are near his heart (Jud 8:25-27).

A test is part of faith, as Christ himself repeats: "Every branch that does bear fruit he prunes to make it bear even more" (Jn 15:2). Abraham's test was particularly severe. The three days that Abraham spent on his way to the place of sacrifice were without doubt the most agonizing days of his life. This God in whom he had placed his trust was only a very newly found friend; Abraham did not yet know him well. He had been reared in the paganism of Mesopotamia, where human sacrifice was not uncommon, and it could well be that this new God of his, whose name he did not even know, was not so very different from the gods of his early years. In Hebrew thought a name assumes tremendous importance, but it was not until the time of Moses that God revealed his name to men. Until that time he was simply "the God of Abraham, the God of Isaac;" he was still the unknown God, and Abraham in this, his moment of supreme trial, had no one to whom he could turn for guidance. In matters of faith he is the pioneer, and the only thing he really knows is that this unknown God is reliable. Perhaps this is the essence of faith: to be convinced of the reliability of God.

For the moment, however, Abraham is all but bewildered, filled with terrible emotions, the dismay that a father experiences at the deathbed of a beloved son. In Abraham's case the suffering was intensified by the knowledge that he could avoid it merely by disobeying the command of his new God. It is alleged that during the Second World War the son of a well known German physicist was active in the Resistance Movement, and eventually he was captured by the Nazis, who offered to the father the release of the son on condition that the father would make a public statement of loyalty to the Nazi regime. The father's response was like Abraham's: he would not go against his conscience even to save the life of his son. As Abraham journeys with Isaac to the mount of sacrifice, his suffering is increased with every step. Isaac as yet knows nothing of the impending tragedy. In the loaded silence of their journey there ensued the little dialogue, terse, uncomplicated by explanations or conjectures. Isaac spoke to his father Abraham: "Father," he said, and with immense tenderness Abraham replied, "Yes, my son." Then came the question of the boy who had grown uneasy, sensing that something was amiss: "Look," he said, "here are the fire and the wood, but where is the lamb for the burnt offering?" Abraham replied, "My son,

God himself will provide the lamb for the burnt offering."
What conflicts are implied in this answer! Let us not say
too glibly that these words are an expression of trust in
God; they are that, of course, but it is so easy to
underestimate the depth of this answer. It is easy to miss
the anguish hidden in its brevity. Abraham does not yet
know how the horrible event is going to end. We do—and
that is the tremendous difference. Abraham, who really
wants to do what God asks, loves his son dearly. Ironically,
his love for God has grown because of this son who was
God's gift to him, and now it is precisely this very gift
which God is asking of him. Abraham is completely
confused. "God himself will provide the lamb for the
burnt offering" is a cry of despair, like the weeping of a
man who can no longer hold back his tears. It is a cry of
confidence also, but a confidence at once painful and very
arduous.

"Then the two of them went on together." At this
point neither knew what was to come. Faith does not
mean that we know all the answers; it does mean that we
are not afraid of the questions, that we have the courage to
let the questions really be asked. Any repression of this
kind is always a lack of faith. Faith implies that we have
the strength and the courage to carry on even when we do
not know the answers, but are just stimulated by a vague
surmise that question and riddle are not the only realities.
To be really confused and not to know where we are
going, even to experience serious doubt can very well be
part of faith; as a matter of fact, it is trials of this kind
which are so often found in biblical faith. In this respect
the psalms are instructive for us: they never repress
anything; they express all, bringing to God their difficulties, their loss of confidence, their doubts. All this is very
healthy; it is the only way to cope with existential
questions, but even as we lay them before God we know

17

that we may not receive answers immediately. Faith is an attitude acquired only slowly, gradually, through many crises and darknesses. It may be that the certitude that the crisis is not necessarily a loss is really the conviction of faith: "We know that by turning everything to their good God co-operates with all those who love him" (Rom 8:28). Indeed, every crisis can be fruitful, as St. Thérèse of Lisieux recognized when at the end of her life she remarked, "Everything is a grace!" To speak like this when you are dying at twenty-three is indeed the fullness of faith, helping us to view even difficult realities so that their goodness shines out.

We know how Abraham's ordeal ended, how Yahweh does not want human sacrifices as did the gods of the neighboring people. We even understand that the whole point of the story is to bring home to us that God does not want us to die, but to live and to thrive, and that a putting to the test of my faith may be the means whereby true knowledge of God deepens. God is never a threat. Abraham's crisis brings this truth out clearly and helps us to understand that even in what may seem an unbelievably difficult demand God is never menacing us. Such is not his way. It is possible that for a variety of reasons in our past experiences we have come to a point where there is far too much negativism in our faith. Perhaps we do not love ourselves enough. There must be mortification in our lives, it is true, but even in this there must be the strong conviction that God wants us to grow and prosper and be happy. In the delicate matter of self-scrutiny for the eradication of faults it is easy to miss the balance and by over-emphasis on failings to distort the healthy self-image which alone makes enthusiastic effort possible. Any counselor experienced with persons who have been sub-jected to the wrong kind of introspection and censure can tell of the debilitating effect this distortion has on the inner growth of the subject, who often finds it difficult to look openly and honestly at his failings and then do something about them. The converse is also true, of course. Where the person has a realistic and positive self-concept, he can make progress no matter what his failings. A robust spirit of faith helps us to achieve this balance. The story of Abraham is there to bring home to us in a striking, almost emotional way, that our God wants us to live and not to die, to grow and prosper and not to wither.

When Abraham descends from the mountain with his son, both he and Isaac have changed; something has happened on that hilltop. Bonhoeffer says they have turned 360°; that is, as far as one can see, they are still in the same position. Nothing seems to have changed. But there *has* been change. Like a tree which has been turned full circle in the ground, Abraham's roots have been cut loose, and he has returned a new man. An outsider, looking upon him as he came down the hill, would have seen no difference, but he is truly different; an inner transformation has taken place. This is the work of faith. For the man of faith, God is truly the ultimate, and therefore, he is a God who keeps him always on the move. A book by Erich Pzrywara, S.J., expresses this well in its title: *Deus semper maior*—God is always greater. I must always keep moving, always making the response of faith: to leave behind, to go up, to carry on if I want to be a person of faith. That flourishing of faith, leaving Ur of the Chaldeans, is a continual reality in the life of one who believes.

There is a final point to the story of Abraham: what happened to Abraham and Isaac is very clearly a fore-shadowing of the New Testament: "Abraham was confident that God had the power even to raise the dead; and so, figuratively speaking, he was given back Isaac from the dead" (Heb 11:19). "Figuratively speaking" points to someone who really did come back from the dead. Jesus is the fulfillment of Abraham's story. We can never really understand the Old Testament unless through Christ, since it is only in Christ that the Old Testament opens and becomes transparent in its real meaning. St. Paul makes this point very strongly:

> ...the minds of the Israelites had been dulled; indeed, to this very day, that same veil is still there when the old covenant is being read, a veil never lifted, since Christ alone can remove it. Yes, even today, whenever Moses is read, the veil is over their minds. It will not be removed until they turn to the Lord (2 Cor 3:14-16).

The story of Abraham is one of many examples of this fulfillment in Christ. We cannot understand the point of the Abraham story unless we keep in mind Christ risen from the dead. The Jesus who comes from Golgotha, like Abraham and Isaac, has turned 360°. He is the same Jesus, and yet is completely different: the risen Lord. Isaac and Jesus, in a unique way, are both only sons. Both have been born in a miraculous way; both have themselves carried the wood for their sacrifice; both are sacrificed on top of a hill: Golgotha and Moriah, at a distance of a ten-minutes' walk from one another; and both have survived the ordeal. Isaac, of course, is merely a foreshadowing. In Jesus we have the full reality, so Jesus is indeed the fulfillment of Abraham's faith (see Jn 8:56-58). In Christ we can fully see how true it is that God wants us to live. That is the message of the new covenant—God wants us to live not just for sixty or eighty or a hundred years, not just for a lifetime, but forever. That shows the earnestness of God's longing for our life and happiness. The realization of this is what faith is all about.

Two

A WOMAN OF FAITH

Abraham, the father of all believers, finds his counter-part in Mary, the first believer of the New Testament. When we consider Mary as a woman of faith, we recognize in her that same basic attitude of belief which we are striving for, and we feel a certain kinship with her. For Mary as for us what the letter to the Hebrews says holds true: "Only faith can guarantee the blessings that we hope for or prove the existence of the realities that at present remain unseen" (11:1).

Some years ago in their pastoral letter on Mary the bishops of Holland reminded us that it is good always to begin our reflection on the person of Mary by pondering her faith, realizing that she, more than anyone else, is a believer, a woman of faith. In this the bishops were following Vatican II, which described Mary in "her pilgrimage of faith," (LG 58), pointing out that "she stands out among the poor and humble of the Lord who confidently await and receive salvation from him" (LG 55). Here the Council is taking up a tradition of the early Middle Ages which stressed Mary's faith, giving more emphasis to it than to her divine maternity. When in the twelfth century St. Bernard wrote: *Virgo credidit et credendo Virgo concepit*, i.e., the Virgin believed and in her faith the Virgin conceived, he was affirming the same belief which had led St. Augustine in the fourth century to coin the famous dictum: *Prius mente concepit quam ventre*, i.e., she first conceived him in her heart before conceiving him in her womb.

In fact, one can say that the Christian writers of the first four centuries paid more attention to the unique act of faith of Mary at the annunciation than to the revelation of her divine motherhood at the nativity. In the last analysis, this tradition is rooted in the New Testament itself, where all texts giving substantial information on the life of Mary actually speak about her words and deeds as a believer. Mary is praised because of her faith: "Blessed is she who believed" (Lk 1:45).

Two examples from Luke and one from John illustrate well this point.

> Now as Jesus was speaking, a woman in the crowd raised her voice and said, 'Happy the womb that bore you and the breasts you sucked!' But he replied, 'Still happier those who hear the word of God and keep it!' (Lk 11:27-28)

To understand this text we have to remember that in the Old Testament one blesses or curses a person by blessing or cursing that person's parents. At first the response of Christ may sound like an insult to his mother. In fact, it is a far more profound praise of her than the woman in the crowd had given. Christ reinforces and deepens the tribute to his mother: Do not bless her because of something physical, but rather because she has heard the Word of God and has kept it and lived for it. Who heard and kept the Word of God more than Mary?

In Luke again we find a similar text:

> His mother and his brothers came looking for him, but they could not get to him because of the crowd. He was told, 'Your

mother and brothers are standing outside and want to see you.' But he said in answer, 'My mother and my brothers are those who hear the word of God and put it into practice' (Lk 8:19-21).

No one heard the Word of God more than Mary; she opened herself completely to it. No one put it into practice more than she; through her it became flesh. In the verse before this one Jesus had warned: ". . .take care how you hear." Mary is the perfect example of how to hear. "I am the handmaid of the Lord, let what you have said be done to me" (Lk 1:38); this is Mary's way of hearing, through which the Word became God-with-us.

We find the third example in John's gospel (2:4-5):

. . .the mother of Jesus said to him, 'They have no wine.' Jesus said, 'Woman, why turn to me? My hour has not come yet.' His mother said to the servants, 'Do whatever he tells you,'

At first glance there seems something rather puzzling about the sequence of events at Cana. Mary, recognizing a need of her friends, came to Jesus, fully confident of his ability to help, yet Jesus seemed almost to repulse her: "My hour has not come yet." But immediately Christ gave to the embarrassed host jars brimming over with splendid wine, proving thereby that in spite of his words his hour had indeed come. What was it that made the difference and drew forward the hour? We find the answer in Mary's simple admonition: "Do whatever he tells you." Here was a heart and a will entirely open to God as it had been at Nazareth when she was ready to accept all, as it had been during all the years when she had pondered in her heart the meaning of her son and had come to recognize him and to accept him as God's word spoken to men. It is when God finds such openness and such receptivity that he can truly be God, that he can bring his kingdom among men and show the first of its signs. At Cana Mary showed us the way of faith, for to recognize the Word of God in Christ and to live by it: in the New Testament this is what constitutes faith.

Mary's response to the message of the annunciation was a simple surrendering of herself wholly to a life of faith. At that moment she gave herself completely to the Word of God, a Word which she had not yet fully grasped but on which she was prepared to base her life. This attitude of faith demanded of Mary is biblical in the highest sense of the word. Not only has she to assent to an absolute reality, a kind of first principle, as people do when they say, "I believe that there must be something at the origin of the universe." This is faith, of course, but it is rather meager. What is demanded of Mary is much more. Nor had she merely to accept as true a specific doctrine, believing on the cognitive level. Further, what is asked of her is more than mere commitment to sacred ritual: certain laws to be observed from this time on. Essentially, what is demanded is an acknowledgment that God is present and active here and now; and she must give her personal cooperation with this divine activity. Faith thus becomes personal, realistic, committing. Mary believed that God had called her; she surrendered herself to that call and followed him into the unknown. She did not yet know where the Word of God would lead her, but she was prepared to put her whole life at stake. We recognize here the same picture as that of Abraham: a call of God, no guarantee, only a promise. But that is enough to cause Abraham to leave his tribe and his country and to go forth into an unknown country. We are here touching the very core of faith: to believe in a personal God who calls me and leads me. In her act of faith Mary placed at God's disposal not just her mind and heart, but her body as well. This act of faith was to shape in a most intimate way her whole life as a human being and as a woman. For her, faith was not something abstract, something merely interior; it was existential, all-embracing, encompassing everything that life might offer.

Mary had been educated in the Old Testament. In a sense, we can say that she was both its summary and its summit. At the same time, she is the beginning of the New. She has been reared in that religious tradition in which God seemed far away, aloof in his infinite majesty. The very term KABOD, signifying the crushing majesty of God, is a typical key-word used to describe the God of Israel. When Moses approached the burning bush, God called to him: "Come no nearer. Take off your shoes, for the place on which you stand is holy ground. I am the God of your father" (Ex 3:5-6). Later, when the time for the covenant had come, the people had to prepare themselves for two days; then "at daybreak on the third day there were peals of thunder on the mountain and lightning flashes, a dense cloud, and a loud trumpet blast, and inside the camp all the people trembled" (Ex 19:16). From then onward the luminous cloud during the day and the pillar of fire at night were the signs of God's presence until the temple was built as Yahweh's dwelling place, the most magnificent, most impressive edifice the Jews had known. This majesty of God was so tremendous that no human being could survive seeing God. Even Moses, who asked to see the face of God, was denied this privilege: "You cannot see my face, for man cannot see me and live" (Ex 33:20).

CALLED BY NAME

In the vision which accompanied the call of the prophet Isaiah, we hear the prophet exclaim: "What a wretched state I am in! I am lost, for. . .my eyes have looked at the King, Yahweh Sabaoth" (Is 6:5). Even a picture or a statue of Yahweh would have been utterly blasphemous: Yahweh is so tremendous that no image could ever do him justice. Reverence for God's grandeur was such that not even his name might be pronounced. Whenever the sacred letters YHWH occurred in the holy books, they were always replaced in pronunciation by the word *Adonai*. True, YHWH is the name which God himself had revealed at the burning bush; but it is a name too holy to be pronounced by human lips.

There is an incident in the history of the chosen people which epitomizes well this concept of the awe-inspiring greatness of Yahweh. After their victory over the Philistines, the Jews had carried back to Jerusalem in solemn procession the Ark of the Covenant.

> David and all the House of Israel danced before Yahweh with all their might. . . .When they came to the threshing-floor of Nacon, the priest Uzzah stretched his hand out to the ark of God and steadied it, as the oxen were making it tilt. Then the anger of Yahweh blazed out against Uzzah, and for this crime God struck him down on the spot, and he died there beside the ark of God (2 Sam 6:5-7).

Mary had been reared in this reverence for the awesome majesty of God. Her parents and teachers had imbued her with a deep respect for the unassailable greatness of God and his infinite distance above our lowly human condition. Eagerly she had drunk in this sacred instruction. And yet, it is with Mary that the New

26

Testament begins. From now on, God is no longer infinitely remote in his tremendous majesty, but very close in his human helplessness, and it is in the person of Mary that this change comes about. Think of the utter transformation of faith demanded when God becomes man! The very structure of faith is intrinsically altered. Zealous herself in the Old Testament way of belief, Mary had to help this little baby in all those things which a mother does for a child. At times today one meets people who complain that there are so many changes in the Church, so many certainties have vanished. This always makes me smile. Think of Mary and the changes she had to experience! Yet she did not complain, but quietly, graciously, made the transition. The Jews had expected a messiah born of man and adopted by God. Actually, God sent a messiah born of God and become man. And Mary was the first to absorb this turning upside down of the Jewish faith-tradition.

The centenary book for the foundation of the Society of Jesus, *Imago primi saeculi*, 1640, has a famous epitaph for St. Ignatius from an anonymous Flemish Jesuit scholastic: *Non coerceri maximo, contineri tamen a minimo, divinum est*; i.e., not to be encompassed by the greatest yet to let oneself be encompassed by the smallest—that is divine. The whole universe is too small for God—the Old Testament had stressed this; yet God was contained in the little infant of Bethlehem and in the man Jesus—this is emphasized by the New Testament. In Mary these two apparently contradictory insistences meet, and her faith was deep enough to encompass them both.

It may well be that the faith of the New Testament is more difficult than the faith of the Old. A God who is close to us in his incarnation puts our faith more to the test than a God who is far away in transcendent majesty. It is the human element more than the divine which we find difficult to accept. We know that in the Church as the Body of Christ the incarnation is prolonged. In its own way and on its own level we encounter there again a human—sometimes an all too human—reality which at the same time constitutes God's presence among us, and it may be that the frailty of the human element obscures at times the very real presence of the divine. At such times it is well to remember Mary, the first of the new faith, the first to recognize and to accept the divine in the human.

From the moment of the annunciation Mary began an unknown future. Like Abraham she set out not knowing where she was going, having nothing to hold on to but the Word of God. At some time or other we have all experienced the human tendency to sketch out definite lines of faith so that we may know explicitly where we are going. But faith eludes such certainty. It means that we cannot grasp, cannot cling to anything. There is always a setting out to be accomplished. We must always leave something behind and not look back. If we refuse to keep moving, if we insist upon holding to something tangible, we narrow down our faith, and that means unbelief. It was this narrowing-down of faith which caused the death of Christ. On Calvary he died because he had not corresponded to the picture of the messiah which the Pharisees had cherished. The scribes had claimed to know what the messiah would be like, but when the Son of God came into the world, they killed him because they persisted in their own expectations rather than accept the reality of God—made-man.

True faith is always open, always ready to grow: "There is no eternal city for us in this life" (Heb 13:14).

Mary advanced from one surprise to another. Everything in her life seemed different, contrary to what she had expected or even imagined, and all the circumstances of her life demanded of her a response of faith. Of this scripture gives many examples:

> The angel said to Mary: 'You are to conceive and bear a son, and you must name him Jesus. He will be great and will be called Son of the Most High. The Lord God will give him the throne of his ancestor David; he will rule over the House of Jacob forever and his reign will have no end' (Lk 1:32-33).

But when the hour of his birth arrives, she has nowhere to place him but in a manger:

> ...the time came for her to have her child and she gave birth to a son, her first-born. She wrapped him in swaddling clothes, and laid him in a manger because there was no room for them at the inn (Lk 2:7).

The shepherds have things to say which are a joy for Mary's heart:

> When they saw the child they repeated what they had been told about him, and everyone who heard it was astonished at what the shepherds had to say. As for Mary, she treasured all these things and pondered them in her heart (Lk 2:18-19).

But then, these words are soon completed by the ominous words of Simeon:

> Simeon blessed the child's father and mother and said to Mary his mother, 'You see this child: he is destined for the fall and for the rising of many in Israel, destined to be a sign that is rejected—and a sword will pierce your own soul too—so that the secret thoughts of many may be laid bare' (Lk 2:33-34).

When after three days of anxious search Mary and Joseph found their son in the temple, "they were overcome when they saw him" (Lk 2:48). But the very moment in which they found him became the moment in which they lost him forever, for immediately Jesus told his parents that his real home is with his Father: "Did you not know that I must be in my Father's house?" And the echo of their gnawing pain is heard in Luke's comment: "They did not understand what he meant" (Lk 2:50).

Time and again Mary had to say farewell to her son. He seemed always to draw a line, a kind of frontier between himself and his mother. We may be inclined to smooth away these instances, yet they reveal much more surely the greatness of Mary than do all the pious exaggerations of a mindless devotion. From them we see how her son was always beyond her. She could not really understand, let alone grasp him; always he was greater than she had thought. Yet accepting her inability to understand fully, she consented to his self-concept. Having pondered his mystery in her heart, she followed him where he led and thus let her life be shaped by him. Ever at the disposal of God's Word, Mary was truly a woman of faith. Eventually all this will bring her to Calvary: "Near the cross of Jesus stood his mother. . ." (Jn 19-25). More than anyone else she shares the death of her son. This separation by death is part of the divine mystery of Jesus continually eluding his mother. It is the final implication of her *fiat* to all that the angel had left unexplained, all that Mary had had to find out in a lifetime. When she leaves Calvary, she is a thoroughly lonely woman, but still a woman of faith. A Dominican litany of the thirteenth century contains the lovely invocation: "Holy Mary, who kept the faith on Holy Saturday, pray for us." It was just this faith which made her lonely. When Jesus died the death of a criminal, even his best friends, his most faithful followers abandoned all hope. There was no longer any one of them who believed in him. Mary alone kept faith between the death and the resurrection. Once again the comparison between Mary and Abraham becomes striking: at a given point in time both were the only believers in the whole world.

After the appearances of the risen Lord and his ascension Mary joined the disciples in prayer in the upper room: "All these joined in continuous prayer, together with several women, including Mary the mother of Jesus..." (Acts 1:14). This, the last of the more than forty times Mary is mentioned in scripture, describes her in an attitude typical of her: inspiring with her faith and her prayer the community of the early Church. She continues to do what she has always done: to be open to the Word of God become flesh through her.

At the end of her life when she has faithfully accomplished everything that had been implied in her *fiat*, she is once more surprised by the God in whom she has believed. A life-time of faith has created in her an immense receptivity. All this is filled now to the brim when God lets her share the glory of her risen son. As she had been the first in many other instances, she is now the first to attain the last goal: filled in body, mind, and soul by the life of the resurrection, she is assumed into that heaven where her faith is raised to total vision.

Gerard Manley Hopkins, S.J., has summarized in a few brief lines the life of Mary:

Mary Immaculate,
...who

This one work has to do—
Let all God's glory through
God's glory which would go
Through her and from her flow
Off, and no way but so.

Indeed, she did let all God's glory through; nothing was sifted out because she was pure as crystal, immaculate in her conception. Like thirsting soil she was open and receptive, an expectancy formed in the age-old history of her people longing for the revelation of God's glory among them. And because she was transparent, the fullness of God's glory did come through her and into this world:

The Word was made flesh,
he lived among us
and we saw his glory (Jn 1:14).

Like freshly fallen snow on the mountains she lifted her gaze to God alone; and under the rays of this Sun she became life-giving water for the valleys below.

Three

THE MAN FOR OTHERS

In our meditations on Christ we must start with the man Jesus, not making him into a superman, but considering how he was wholly one of us, and how his life was like ours in everything except sin—normal, ordinary, lowly, at times wearisome, always very human. We have all met people who never seem tired. Bursting with energy, they never betray weariness and are able to live in a constant frenzy of activity. With Christ this was not so. Possibly one of his most appealing pictures is the incident of the well in Samaria where he shows himself so tired out by the hot, dusty trip that he is forced to sit at the side of the well to rest and to beg a cup of water from the woman who had made herself notorious in her little town. All this was very human, and helps us to realize how nothing human was alien to Christ. And it is noteworthy that the very actions for which he was most frequently criticized were the actions which showed him most a man. When he asked the drink from the Samaritan woman, there were those, undoubtedly, who said: he is not very mortified, asking a drink like this. John the Baptist had come neither eating nor drinking, and people had complained that he was too severe. But when the Son of Man came, and he did eat and drink, these same people complained, "Look, a glutton and a drunkard, a friend of tax collectors and sinners" (Mt 11:18-19).

CALLED BY NAME

It is strange how unrealistic we tend to become in our attempt to re-create the real Jesus. We seem so ready to accept a Christ who was always controlled, never disturbed, never angry. But this is not the Christ of the gospel. There we see a man whose indignation at times blazes forth even against his own disciples, for they more than others were called to understand "the things of God." When Peter a little pompously declared that the harsh things Christ was foretelling of his Passion should never come to pass, Christ did not hesitate to reprove him roundly: "Get behind me, Satan! You are an obstacle in my path, because the way you think is not God's way but man's" (Mt 16:23). His indignation was spontaneous and very obvious when he reproved his apostles for holding back the people who were thronging to him with their little ones: "Let the little children come to me. . . ." (Mk 10:14). His anger was particularly vehement against those who attempted to come between God and man, who tried either to ensnare Jesus when he was bringing to men the healing power of God or to divert men from the service of God. I would not like to have been in the temple courtyard that morning when Christ drove out the buyers and sellers: "Making a whip out of some cord, he drove them all out of the temple, cattle and sheep as well, scattered the money-changers' coins, knocked their tables over, and said to the pigeon-sellers, 'Take all this out of here and stop turning my Father's house into a market'" (Jn 2:15-17). His strongest anger was reserved for those who under a show of religious fervor would have prevented him from bringing aid to the suffering:

He went again into a synagogue, and there was a man there who had a withered hand. And they were watching him to see

34

if he would cure him on the sabbath day, hoping for something to use against him. He said to the man with the withered hand, 'Stand up out in the middle!' Then he said to them, 'Is it against the law on the sabbath day to do good, or to do evil; to save life, or to kill?' But they said nothing. Then, grieved to find them so obstinate, he looked angrily round at them, and said to the man, 'Stretch out your hand.' He stretched it out and his hand was better (Mk 3:1-5).

Even in his suffering Christ was not grandiose. He ended his life as he had begun it, as he had lived it day after day. It had been a hard life. He had never known luxury. He had been born in a stable because his parents could not afford a place in the inn. At death he had nothing but the clothes on his back, and he was stripped even of these. And between these two terminals he lived a life which he characterized: "Foxes have holes and the birds of the air have nests, but the Son of Man has nowhere to lay his head" (Lk 9:58). At times we hear the death of Socrates compared with the death of Christ. Both had been teachers of men; both had been set upon by those who would not accept their teaching; both were put to death. But what a vast difference in the manner of their deaths! After Socrates had had his trial and the verdict had been passed that he was to drink poison, standing forth, he gave a very beautiful speech—impressive, lofty, a final summation of his doctrine. Then he drank the poison. That was the death of a hero. Christ did not die as a hero, however, but as a poor, weak, human creature. He cried out, sweated blood, experienced emptiness, and felt abandoned.

On the other hand, it would be wrong to see in Christ one who did not understand human joys. Nowhere in the gospel do we see him turning in scorn from the ordinary pleasures of life. He was having a good time at the wedding in Cana—in fact, he made more wine, gallons of it, just so that the guests could continue their celebration. He had friends among the propertied: Nicodemus, Joseph of Arimathaea, Zacchaeus, Matthew, his friends of Bethany, the wealthy ladies who "provided for them out of their own resources" (Lk 8:3). But nowhere in the gospel is there an indication that he sought out these wealthy friends in preference to the poor; nowhere do we see him ingratiating himself with the men of rank or money. His sensitive heart responded to human need wherever he encountered it. The grief of the widow of Nain was too much for him; even without a spoken request he restored the youth to his mother. In Bethany we see him in the full vigor of his manhood standing at the tomb of Lazarus, weeping because he has lost his friend. When the rich young man presented himself, inquiring about a yet more perfect way, the sensitive Jesus responded immediately as he looked steadily at him and loved him.

Human misery in any form always called forth a sympathetic response in Christ. The lot of the sick and the handicapped he took to heart, and always he was there to take the part of the poor and the oppressed. He showed a positive solidarity with these, fulfilling the words of the psalmist:

> He will free the poor man who calls to him,
>   and those who need help,
> he will have pity on the poor and feeble,
>   and save the lives of those in need;

he will redeem their lives from exploitation and outrage,
their lives will be precious in his sight (Ps 72:12-14).

Possibly one of the most characteristic qualities of
Christ was this ability of his to live for others. In the words
of Paul: "Christ did not think of himself" (Rom 15:3): he
was truly a man for others. And in this self-forgetfulness
he was carrying out most completely his mission of being
Emmanuel, finding himself because he had lost himself so
fully, according to his own admonition: ". . .anyone who
wants to save his life will lose it; but anyone who loses his
life for my sake will find it" (Mt 16:25). It is this lack of
concern about himself which is so typical of Christ,
constituting, as it were, his very identity. It is the secret of
his love for the people, his total availability to them in
their need. It is not that he was maudlin or weak,
betraying a sentimentality that repels. On the contrary, it
was because he was sensitive to them that he could relate
to them so beautifully, attending to them, listening.

It is interesting how much we betray ourselves in our
own attitude of listening. To listen truly means to make an
other person the center of our association. When I speak, I
am in the middle, and that is easy: I can speak for hours.
When I listen, the other person is in the center, and it is to
him that I must direct my attention. This, however, is
much harder, for I find myself wanting to interject a
comment, a reflection. In fact, after a short time I find
myself no longer listening, but only waiting for the pause
that will make possible my speaking. If I am polite, I do
wait for the opportune moment; if I am impolite, I break
in abruptly. But in either case I have stopped giving full
attention to my friend as he speaks; I am absorbed in my
own response, and all that he is saying goes for nothing.

With Christ, this was not so because he really cared for the other. It was the other in whom he was interested, not himself. And his companions sensed this. They knew that in his presence they could be themselves, need not be concerned. This was part of the liberating influence they found in Christ's presence, part of the power they recognized as coming from him: "...everyone in the crowd was trying to touch him because power came out of him that cured them all" (Lk 6:19). We must not think of this power emanating from Christ as of some kind of mysterious ether or fluidum emanating from him. The truth is much more simple. Luke explains it after his account of the cure of Peter's mother-in-law: "At sunset all those who had friends suffering from diseases of one kind or another brought them to him, and laying his hands on each he cured them" (Lk 4:40). While Jesus is laying his hands on each person, he is not at the same time looking around or chatting with someone else, but his full attention and his whole love flow to that one person, who is thus cured.

The central miracle of the gospel is not this or any other marvelous action evoked by the power of Christ. The miracle of the gospel is Christ himself, the love of God embodied in Jesus Christ. When we really take time to contemplate the harmony and sympathy of his personality, we shall have an overwhelming experience, for in him we encounter God. Theologians sometimes dispute whether or not man can truly experience God. In Christ we can. No other sign is given but the sign of the Son of Man. That is enough! We must be on our guard, however, lest we miss the woods for the trees. Occasionally we meet people who seem to know everything concerning form criticism, redaction criticism, structuralism, *ipsissima verba,* life-setting (*Sitz im Leben*), etc., but have never truly encountered the Person of Christ. They have missed the whole point of biblical exegesis and of revelation. Recently a Trappist from Holland gave testimony how he after twenty-one years of Trappist life discovered Christ:

> Only then Jesus Christ became a living person for me. Twenty-one years I have prayed and meditated with the monks of the abbey, hours and hours of the day and night. I was ordained and said Mass innumerable times. And yet: was he alive for me? Was he a living person for me? I hope that I do not shock or scandalize anybody: he was really an unknown person for me.

Yet the Person of Christ is what the whole gospel is about. The gospel does not present a doctrine, an ideal, or an ideology; it presents Jesus Christ.

It may be that at times we are using the complexities of scholarly theology as a facade behind which we can take refuge. Kierkegaard mocks this when he says:

> We artful dodgers act as if we do not understand the New Testament, because we realize full well that we should have to change our way of life drastically. That is why we invented "religious education" and "christian doctrine." Another concordance, another lexicon, a few more commentaries, three other translations, because it is so difficult to understand. Yes, of course, dear God, all of us—capitalists, officials, ministers, house-owners, beggars, the whole society—we would be lost if it were not for the "scholarly doctrine!"

Actually, the message of Christ is very simple and can be summed up in two phrases: we are loved by God, and that love overflows to our neighbor. Or we can listen simply to the words of Christ: "I was born for this, I came into the world for this: to bear witness to the truth" (Jn 18:37). This truth, in the Old Testament described by the Hebrew word *emeth*, is in Jewish thinking the reliability of God's love. Christ lived only for this: to bring home to us the truth that we are loved by God and that this love is to be relied upon no matter what we may do. God loves us as we are, and he always does so: "We may be unfaithful, but he is always faithful, for he cannot disown his own self" (2 Tim 2:13). This message of God's love is the core of the gospel. If we grasp that, we can truly love God in return, and his love will also enable us to love our neighbor. Once I know myself loved by God, my heart is filled with his love and will overflow, for my human heart is too small to contain it all. Then I shall love my neighbor with this very same love. This is the whole message of the gospel, a message so simple and so sound. What I must do really is open my whole heart, my whole life to the message. There is no other way.

Christ never sought human approbation. When the people wanted to make him king, he ran away (Jn 6:15). He refused to be circumscribed by all the boundaries that tradition and convention had created. He saw publicans not as the reprobates which others saw, but as persons for whom he had come, and he was not turned aside by the scandalized reaction of people: you never deal with men of that sort! He dealt with women, even with prostitutes: it was for such that he had come. In acting as he did, Jesus had no intention of provoking or annoying the leaders of Israel. But he had little patience with the rules which the Jews had erected into a sacred tradition. It was God who meant everything to him; there were no idols in his life. Because the Father dominated his life so completely, he could do what no one else dared to do: he grasped the outstretched hand of unclean persons. In all this he does not defend himself; he does not trim away, does not cut corners or water down the doctrine he was proclaiming. He was utterly sincere, true, consistent: "I am the Truth." By his genuineness he disarms his enemies, fascinates his friends. He manages to do what none of us is able to do: he lives completely without a mask. It is a hero who bears armor; a saint is naked. Christ has nothing to defend or hide: "I have come to bring fire to the earth, and how I wish it were blazing already!" (Lk 12:49). With this fire he has managed to kindle some people who in their turn radiate his warmth and his light to their fellow men: Peter, James, John, Paul, Francis of Assisi, Teresa of Jesus, Charles de Foucauld, Teilhard de Chardin, Dietrich Bonhoeffer, Pope John, Mother Teresa of Calcutta. In every century he manages to enkindle some who have true influence on their fellow men. In this way the kingdom of God is built.

H. G. Wells, a historian, has made this curious admission for one of his persuasion, as if in spite of himself he must recognize the transcendent truth about Christ: "I am an historian. I am not a believer. But I must confess, as an historian, this penniless preacher from Galilee is irresistibly the center of history."[1] This observation, of course, is quite literally true. Our very system of reckoning human events clusters about him: dates are either *before Christ* or *in the year of the Lord.* And the system serves merely to emphasize Christ's position as the very center, the focal point of all human activity. As the center of history Christ has an influence transcending that of all other men. We are so accustomed to the recital of his humble *curriculum vitae* that we may gloss over its exciting significance. From his very first appearance in the remote village of an insignificant occupied territory, through all the hidden and ordinary events of a life of poverty and labor, he lived in an obscurity that was total. During all these years nothing happened that would serve to broaden his outlook or to bring him into contact with the excitement and development of the on-going nations. It is ironic—and part of the tragedy with which he is surrounded—that his one contact with the representatives of enlightened Roman civilization was in the court of law which rather summarily abdicated under pressure from the Jewish opposition, and his method of execution was Roman rather than Jewish. Here there was nothing enlightening, nothing promising for the future. His human dignity was trampled upon to such a degree that his very clothing was gambled away as he hung dying and in agony. And yet, in spite of the utter dereliction and failure of his death, this man today is the very core and center of nations, the leader of mankind's progress and evolution.

And what kind of leader is this Christ? He is very exacting: "Once the hand is laid on the plough, no one who looks back is fit for the kingdom of God" (Lk 9:62). He demands singleness of purpose: "Leave the dead to bury their dead; your duty is to go and spread the news of the kingdom of God" (Lk 9:60). He demands a heroism before which human nature quails: ". . .if your eye should cause you to sin, tear it out; it is better for you to enter into the kingdom of God with one eye, than to have two eyes and be thrown into hell. . ." (Mk 9:47). He warns us that a divided loyalty is self-destructive: "No one can be the slave of two masters: he will either hate the first and love the second, or treat the first with respect and the second with scorn. You cannot be the slave both of God and of money" (Mt 6:24). He cautions us on the delusive enticement of desire: ". . .where your treasure is, there will your heart be also" (Mt 6:21). Lest we misunderstand the difficulties of the way, he forewarns: "Enter by the narrow gate, since the road that leads to perdition is wide and spacious, and many take it; but it is a narrow gate and a hard road that leads to life, and only a few find it" (Mt 7:13-14). Anyone preaching a broad way is not preaching the gospel.

All this is very demanding, radical in the sense that it goes to the very root of existence, but it is not fanatical. In the approach that Christ himself takes, we see quite clearly the difference between the radical and the fanatical. Christ never breaks the crushed reed; he never quenches the smoking flax. When he meets human weakness, he is infinitely mild, as only God can be. He can tell the Parable of the Prodigal Son with such effectiveness only because he has been the father of many prodigals, and he understands the son's weakness in the depest recesses of the boy's soul. One of his greatest proofs of radical living appears in those magnificent words from the cross: "Father, forgive them." That is truly the prayer of a radical. A fanatic would have cursed the enemy in the bitterness of his soul; a radical knows better because he knows more deeply. It is this understanding of the human condition more than any other single quality which reveals so completely the nature of Christ's understanding of man:

Come to me, all you who labor and are overburdened, and I will give you rest. Shoulder my yoke and learn from me, for I am gentle and humble in heart, and you will find rest for your souls. Yes, my yoke is easy and my burden light (Mt 11:28-30).

CALLED BY NAME

To experience this humanity of Christ is the main purpose of Christian contemplation, and it is for this reason that we set about meditation and prayer: to know Christ better. Meditation is popular today, but in itself this can be a hazard, for in their absorption in a method, whether Zen or any other, there is danger that some enthusiastic practitioners may lose the real priority of Christian prayer. For the earnest Christian addressing himself to prayer the ultimate value is: to enter ever more deeply into the mystery of Christ, to be wholly absorbed by his love, to respond with greater generosity to his call. It is not the fact of meditation that is important, not the method, but only the heart of it, and that can be only Christ.

For a Christian true prayer concentrates on the Person of Christ. Ignatius at the beginning of every meditation from the second week of the Exercises onwards offers as the grace to be sought: that I may know Christ more intimately, love him more deeply, follow him yet more closely,—that is what meditation is all about. That too is why we turn to scripture for our prayer, so that while looking at him we may find him becoming more and more the center of our prayer, of our love; that we may grow in the honest desire for friendship with Christ as the deepest, most intimate relationship of our life. Then he will truly be the center. Jesus is Lord, the early Christians used to say, and this is what I want: that he may be truly Lord, dominating my whole life, my whole love.

One of the most beautiful expressions of this relationship between Christ and the person who loves him is found in Teilhard de Chardin's *The Mass on the World*, in a prayer addressed to Christ:

The Man for Others

Glorious Lord Christ: the divine influence secretly diffused and active in the depths of matter, and the dazzling centre where all the innumerable fibres of the manifold meet: power as implacable as the world and as warm as life; you whose forehead is of the whiteness of snow, whose eyes are of fire, and whose feet are brighter than molten gold; you whose hands imprison the stars; you who are the first and the last, the living and the dead and the risen again; you who gather into your exuberant unity every beauty, every affinity, every energy, every mode of existence; it is you to whom my being cried out with a desire as vast as the universe, "In truth you are my Lord and my God."[2]

Four

WHO DO YOU SAY I AM?

One of the perplexing characteristics of human nature is our tendency to miss the obvious, to become so involved in ever-growing complexities that we overlook what is central. Like coins, our ideas become thin from over-use, and because the imprint denoting their value is smoothed away, we use them without really understanding their meaning. When this happens in the spiritual life, we miss the single imperative of the gospel on which all others rest: "Set your hearts on his kingdom first, and on his righteousness, and all these other things will be given you as well" (Mt 6:33). In Jesus we are shown what a person is like when God is fully God in his life. He is the perfect realization of the kingdom of God, which forms the core of the gospel message.

Possibly, at first sight the words 'kingdom', 'reign', 'sovereignty', are rather unattractive to us with connotations of force or dominion alien to our culture. But the reality is there to be faced: the key-word 'kingdom of God' is inescapable in the teaching of Jesus. His vision of life gives unconditional priority to the Will of God: "I always do what pleases the Father" (Jn 8:29). The Will of God was the very food that kept him alive (Jn 4:34), and he showed himself absolutely intransigent whenever the Will of his Father was concerned. We must be careful not to whittle down our concept of the Will of God to a size that we can be comfortable with—a kind of efficient means to attain human goals, as one useful element operating among many others for our purposes. It is higher, more awe-inspiring than that, the ultimate by which everything is measured, and being transcendent, it can never itself be subjected to any human value. That God be God has unconditional priority: his kingdom and its righteousness come first, and all other considerations are secondary. But the whole point of the revolution he has brought is to show precisely how the kingdom of God is never at the expense of man, but on the contrary, constitutes his only happiness. The Will of God is precisely this: that man be man to the full. His concern is for our happiness, for the plenitude of our human nature, and for the achievement of perfect peace which will be found only in the unfolding of our whole being. Far from being arbitrary or oppressive, God's kingdom is really that of a God who has bound himself by covenant to man, much as in a marriage both partners pledge themselves to be sources of fulfillment for the other. In fact, it is the unassailable sovereignty of the Father which is the inviolable guarantee that man may truly be himself. God's kingdom reveals something about God *and* about man: about God in his relation to man, and about man in his relation to the deepest Ground of himself. In these relations God is the unrivaled, supreme origin.

Of course, all this is nothing but the content of the covenant of old, where Yahweh and his people constitute the happiness of one another. Yet it is only in Jesus that this content becomes evident and can be truly understood. It is the person of Jesus who is the key to scripture. The many words which God has spoken through the prophets at various times and in different ways find their ultimate meaning only through the one Word which God spoke in

48

the fullness of time. This is one way in which St. Paul establishes the centrality of Jesus Christ. A spirituality that seeks to renew itself, to be radical and authentic, must always find its center in Jesus, and whatever its ramifications, it can never turn aside, but only press ever more surely towards the mark.

Not only does Jesus interpret his Father's kingdom as God's concern for man's happiness; he also lives this teaching: ". . .the kindness and love of God our savior for mankind were revealed" (Tit 3:4). He gives it shape: "I was born for this, I came into the world for this: to bear witness to the truth" (Jn 18:37), where truth means as always in scripture, the reliability of God's love for man as he is. Jesus in his humanity embodies God as loving concern for man. He is the ultimate revelation of God's being, for in him the Father expresses himself fully and flawlessly. Here again we understand what is meant by considering Christ the focal point of all revelation and all spirituality.

From many angles St. Paul develops this centrality of Christ in the life of a Christian. We must take over the mentality of Christ: "In your minds you must be the same as Christ Jesus" (Phil 2:5). We must grow together with him: "I live now not with my own life but with the life of Christ who lives in me" (Gal 2:20). His life is more authentically ours than is our own life. In one sense, we are all split personalities, ever so often alienated even from ourselves. At some time we all betray our identity, doing the exact opposite of what we know to be genuine (Rom 7:14-24). Our life is thus divided, but he *is* life. To live with his life, therefore, is to embrace that way which alone makes it possible for us to be wholly and authentically ourselves. And yet each of us experiences within himself the classic struggle described so vividly in St. Paul. The inauthentic in us strives ceaselessly to resist and reject the life of Christ in us. Between January 2, 1968, when Philip Blaiberg received a new heart during a surgical transplantation, and August 14, 1969, when he died, his entire body, from the brain to the least important cell fought with astounding ferocity and inventiveness to repel the new heart that, nevertheless, was vital for him. In a similar way our old, divided, inauthentic, and yet so real self will resist the life of Christ in us, which, nevertheless, we need absolutely. Because it is an evil threatening our life, that resistance has to be mortified. To absorb the vitality of Christ in ourselves implies pain and darkness, mortification and purification, not because Christ wants to inflict suffering on us, but because the impure and inauthentic in us resist transformation. Long ago the Father, who wants us to live, planned this transformation so that we might become true images of his Son, who would be the eldest of many brothers (cf. Rom 8:29). Here again we have another attempt to emphasize the centrality of Christ for mankind.

We are speaking here not merely of an impersonal, intellectual assent to the dominance of Christ in our life. If our prayer is genuine and persevering, it will lead us inevitably to the assurance that in Christ we find the true pattern of our life, and this certitude is conducive to a more total transformation. It is in Jesus that we find the deepest yearning of our hearts satisfied; in him we perceive the goodness which restlessly we have been seeking. In the intimate revelation of himself to us Christ discloses what it really means to be human, and from him we learn what makes man's life worth while. In one way the deepest mystery of life is lived by Christ in such a way that it can be seen by everybody. But in prayer this revelation becomes personal and real; here the mystery of *my* life is revealed by Jesus, and I recognize this truth with a joyful sense of wonder. I need no longer doubt nor grope; Christ has made manifest what is meant by humanness and has shown me the way to achieve it. The transformation thus effected is deep and all-pervasive. We become fascinated by him, and much that at one time seemed important in our lives pales before the radiance of Christ: "...I believe nothing can happen that will outweigh the supreme advantage of knowing Christ Jesus my Lord. For him I have accepted the loss of everything, and I look on everything as so much rubbish if only I can have Christ and be given a place in him" (Phil 3:8).

Perhaps we can express this experience in something like a syllogism. God is the deepest Ground of our being, the most intimate mystery of our existence, the very heart of our ego. This God has become incarnate in Jesus. In him, therefore, the deepest mystery of our own life is disclosed and made accessible. It is this realization which fills us with that deep peace which the world can never give and which binds us all the more closely to Christ. He clarifies our life, makes it transparent, gives it new perspective.

In elementary physics there is a little experiment to make visible with the help of iron filings on cardboard the lines of force of a magnetic field. In similar fashion we can say that the life of Christ makes visible the lines of force of human life. Let us examine a few of these lines of force in the life of Christ which are typical of any human life.

There was, first of all, the total availability of Christ. He was truly a man for others, their property, so to speak. There was room for all, and each one approaching him found a warm welcome. There was no question of his trying to use people, to manipulate them, to enjoy himself at their expense. Rather, he devoted himself to each one personally, intensely, and he received each one as he was. No one was unimportant in his eyes. He had genuine interest in the real self of the other, and as a result, in his presence every man could be himself. Moreover, nothing human was unimportant to him; he could enter wholly into the joys and needs of the people, and this so universally that no man seemed "impossible" for him. Jesus even went so far as to pray for his executioners at the very moment in which they were thoroughly enjoying the "good work" they were doing for the "glory of God", mercilessly mocking him in his pain and shame. Indeed, no one was left unaccepted by Jesus. When Mother Teresa of Calcutta with her extensive, personal experience of human misery, maintains that the worst suffering is the feeling of not being accepted or wanted, and that this disease is the one which ultimately she tries to cure, she shows herself a faithful disciple of her Master, who twenty centuries earlier gave everybody the certainty that he was wholly and unconditionally accepted.

Perhaps we may have envied the apparent ease with which Jesus was able to relate so beautifully to people with a sensitive and sincere love. We may wonder what was the secret of this ability. How could he manage? His secret is to be found on every page of the gospel: Christ's total orientation was to his Father. Let him speak for only five minutes, and you will be sure to find that his Father has entered the picture. For him his Father meant everything. The favor of the Father was the air he breathed. The experience of his Father was the very source whence he drew his life. Without this Abba-experience, the life and message of Jesus become an empty myth, robbed of any existential value or meaning. To speak about Jesus without adverting to his profound and most fruitful relation to his Father is to betray him in the very heart of his existence, for beyond all else he finds his joy and security in his Father. As a result, he lives secure in his Father's acceptance, and there is not the slightest self-concern in him. Here we can identify the link between his relation with his Father and his relations with men. Being so completely at home with his Father, he had no need to be concerned about himself and he could devote full attention and undivided love to the people. Because his roots sank so deep in his Father, his branches could reach out so far to all men. The love which he experienced from his Father was the secret of his own charity for others. The realization of this connection between God's love for us and our love for each other discloses part of the mystery of our life and helps us to relate more authentically to our neighbor in himself and in his need.

There is a second fundamental feature of the mystery of human existence clearly revealed in the life of Jesus. To grasp fully this trait requires a revolution somewhat comparable to that experienced by the human mind when in the sixteenth century Copernicus and Galilei demonstrated that not the earth, but the sun was the center of the then known universe. (Today we have to correct even this statement and reduce the sun to the modest function of constituting the center of just our solar system, thereby minimizing the position of the earth immensely more than the sixteenth century did.) In its day, however, the adjustment required by these astronomers was revolutionary. How much more revolutionary was the re-orientation demanded by Jesus when he led us to admit that we are not the center of our own life! Difficult though this truth may appear at first, it is also very liberating: "For anyone who wants to save his life will lose it; but anyone who loses his life for my sake will find it" (Mt 16:25). Once we make Christ the center of our lives, everything seems to fall into place, and perspective, harmony, and peace follow. After some time mankind adjusted itself to the Copernican revolution so that today it would be difficult to find any serious rejection of the thesis. The Christian revolution, however, always remains revolutionary, for there remains always the tendency to focus on self; there is still so much talk of self-fulfillment, self-protection, self-determination, self-decision, self-confidence, self-respect—selfhood! For Jesus the approach is different. He is quite literally *eccentric*, off-center so far as he himself is concerned. For him growth takes place in a freedom from self-concern; success is found in the last place, receiving in giving, life in death.

> I tell you, most solemnly,
> unless a wheat grain falls on the ground and dies,
> it remains only a single grain;
> but if it dies,
> it yields a rich harvest (Jn 12:24).

The central event of his life, his death-and-resurrection, is one large-scale object-lesson of this disconcerting, basic truth: in the cross, glory is found; if we are to live and grow, we must die. Before the paradox of a cross at once life-giving and death-dealing, we find ourselves confronting a reality almost beyond our comprehension. The medieval artist sometimes tried to express this truth by representing the dying Christ on the cross vested in the full regalia of priest or king. It was his attempt to render in artistic medium the Christian revolution.

Who Do You Say I Am?

These are two examples of the way in which Jesus maps out for us the depths hidden in our own lives. In himself he recapitulates human life:

All that came to be had life in him
and that life was the light of men (Jn 1:4).

I am the Way, the Truth and the Life (Jn 14:6).

The life of a man—any man—has reached fulfillment when it resembles the life of Jesus. It is not mediocrity that God wants: the Father desires that we live life to the full, but the only way to this plenitude is to live in the likeness of Christ: "They are the ones he chose specially long ago and intended to become true images of his Son" (Rom 8:29). Where we fail to reproduce this likeness of Christ, we fail before God and man alike. Gandhi used to say, "I like Christ, but I dislike Christians because they are so very unlike Christ." Similarly, a young man in Africa remarked somewhat sadly, "We are fed up with people who bring up Jesus Christ, but we would love to meet one who is really like Jesus." I felt ashamed when I heard this—and yet these words came straight from our own faith. Do we not ourselves profess in our creed that the ultimate criterion for judging a human life is precisely Jesus? "He will come again in glory to judge the living and the dead." Our lives will be compared to his, and that confrontation will decide how authentic our life has been.

The meaning of our lives, then, is found in the imitation of Christ. But this is not just an individual affair. Christ is not yet fully formed, has not yet attained his full growth. The imitation of Christ implies transcending one's individual self by becoming a living member of the total

Christ. This does not imply a loss of personality, but rather a deepening and strengthening of it. "In this way we are all to come to unity in our faith and in our knowledge of the Son of God, until we become the perfect Man, fully mature with the fullness of Christ himself" (Eph 4:13).

Carl Gustav Jung, the famous Swiss psychiatrist, said that one-third of his patients did not suffer from any neurosis or psychosis, but rather from the meaninglessness of life (and he sometimes added that two-thirds of this group were over forty). A confirmation of this thesis seems to be found in the work of Viktor E. Frankl, the Jewish psychiatrist from Vienna, who spent three years in the concentration camps of Auschwitz and Dachau. Frankl bases his whole psychiatry on "man's search for meaning." He calls his school *logo-therapy* because the Greek word *logos* denotes meaning, and his basic thesis holds that the striving to find a meaning in one's life is the primary motivational force in man. A Christian is one who has found the total meaning of life in Christ, in following and imitating him, and in growing into the living Christ.

Five

CONTEMPLATIVE IN ACTION

The age-old ideal of being contemplative in action lies at the origin of the Society of Jesus, but no doubt it has a much longer tradition than Ignatius and his early Jesuits. St. Benedict, for example, had never intended a water-tight division between the *ora et labora*, pray and work. Throughout the centuries many persons, fascinated by this synthesis, have worked hard to achieve it. As an army chaplain during World War I William Doyle said an improbable number of ejaculatory prayers each day, but while we marvel at the ardor of his efforts, we wonder whether this is really the way to contemplate in action. The following considerations on prayer rooted in life and life rooted in prayer may help to clarify somewhat this difficult concept.

Five A

PRAYER ROOTED IN LIFE

Authentic prayer is very realistic and has everything to do with the actual situation of our daily life. When at the end of a retreat some people in a voice both determined and relieved say, "Back to reality," I always ask myself (and sometimes them) just how "real" is the reality to which they are returning if it means a break with the prayer-experience they have just had. Does "real" mean "shallow"? Or did they use during their retreat a prayer-coat in which they escaped from real life? There is always the possibility of praying with only part of self, with one of the many subselves at my disposal. But this means a caricature of prayer.

True prayer is very personal—that is to say, it encompasses my whole self. A joy, a grief, or a worry should not be kept out of my prayer. True, the superficialities of life can become a distraction which thwarts contact with God's presence, but anything that eats my heart out should be presented to God. The very fact that it means so much to me implies that in one way or another God has something to do with it, something to say about it. The constraint of trying to blot out all distractions could very well suffocate prayer. To pray does not mean to ignore the things that are real and to see things that are different; it does mean to see the real things in a different way. It means to look with the eye of faith so as to see more easily the deepest Ground of all that is; in other words, to grasp reality more fully and more truly. "Ever since God created the world his everlasting power and deity—however invisible—have been there for the mind to see in the things he has made" (Rom 1:20). "In fact God is not far from any of us, since it is in him that we live, and move, and exist" (Acts 17:27-28). Every object, every person, every situation speaks of God if only we learn to listen. According to the Russian expression repeated so often by Catherine de Hueck Doherty, to pray is to put one's head into one's heart. In this way a new depth of perspective is revealed, and our "cerebral shortsightedness" is cured.

The psalms are beautiful examples of realistic prayer. All deep human emotions find their place somewhere in these songs: community and communion as well as utter loneliness and isolation, deep joy at success and fortune as well as anguish to the point of despair, wonder over a healthy human body and fear of death, faith and adoration as well as doubts and darkness, gratitude and fierce complaints—all these and many other experiences are expressed and brought before God. The psalms are so powerful because they integrate and make whole all that man undergoes. There is no subterfuge in the psalms, no holding back. They really go all the way, yes all the way to the Most High, and from this point we can see the events of life in true perspective.

There is a story told of a young man who, finding prayer difficult, consulted his director about this inability. The guru gave him this advice: "Take a long sheet of paper, or rather, take a roll, and write down every gift that comes to you in the course of a day. But be careful not to take anything for granted." This advice is sound, for it brings prayer back to human experience, the humus layer, as it were, in which authentic prayer takes root. When human experience is thin and shallow, prayer cannot grow. When we take everything too casually, when there is no sense of wonder and no genuine attention to things, to situations, or to people, prayer will become stifled and artificial—that is, if there is any prayer at all. A superficial way of life suffocates all prayer. We need an atmosphere of acknowledging not just intellectually but in our hearts that life is a gift, a manifold and continuous gift. Ingratitude is a fault that avenges itself far more than we can ever realize. When a person forgets to give thanks, prayer and even life itself lose their flavor. That is why the psalm invites: "Bless Yahweh, my soul, and remember all his kindnesses" (Ps 103:2). What should rise spontaneously in us may have to be learned with diligent effort: to thank God. Without gratitude there is no depth to our life.

In the Amsterdam National Museum an elderly couple came to see Rembrandt's masterpiece, "The Nightwatch." When, after a long walk through the many corridors they finally reached the famous painting, the usher overheard the man say to his wife: "Look, what a beautiful frame!" It may be that the frame is indeed fine, but it would seem that some element was missing in their admiration. For many of us it is so easy to fall in love with the frame and to ignore the painting, or to fall in love with the painting and to forget the painter. The world is filled with wonders, but often we are too sated to notice the real ones. When only the sensational can arouse our enthusiasm, something vital is lacking: we have lost the sense of wonder. We may become excited about an Olympic track-race, but overlook the simple fact that we can walk. As St. Augustine remarked in his well known homily on the multiplication of loaves, people are filled with awe because of this miracle, but they take for granted that their own daily food is provided.

Prayer in spirit and in truth means a piercing through the shroud which "common sense" may lay over the mystery of existence. Worship transforms our vision of reality, helping us to realize more surely God's love and care behind the complexities of life. It makes us see as Jesus did how the Father is at work in everything. Then no joy will let us forget the Father who provides, and no worry will separate us from the Father who cares.

> That is why I am telling you not to worry about your life and what you are to eat, nor about your body and how you are to clothe it. Surely life means more than food, and the body more than clothing! Look at the birds in the sky. They do not sow or reap or gather into barns; yet your heavenly Father feeds them. Are you not worth much more than they are? Can any of you, for all his worrying, add one single cubit to his span of life? And why worry about clothing? Think of the flowers growing in the fields; they never have to work or spin; yet I assure you that not even Solomon in all his regalia was robed like one of these. Now if that is how God clothes the grass in the field which is there today and thrown into the furnace tomorrow, will he not much more look after you, you men of little faith? So do not worry... (Mt 6:25-31).

Joy can camouflage our true intent. Kierkegaard tells of the great actor Seydelman, who had been applauded for several minutes after an opera and had been decorated with a wreath. When he returned home, Seydelman gave heart-felt thanks to God for this success. But, Kierkegaard adds reflectively, it was precisely that heart-felt intimacy which revealed that he was not thanking *God*. With the same passion with which he now gave thanks, he would have rebelled against God if he had been booed.

Worry too can and often does distort our prayer:

> God must always be the focus of our attention for there are many ways in which this collectedness may be falsified; when we pray from a deep concern, we have a sense that our whole being has become one prayer and we imagine that we have been in a state of deep, prayerful collectedness, but this is not true, because the focus of attention was not God; it was the object of our prayer. When we are emotionally involved, no alien thought intrudes, because we are completely concerned with what we are praying about; it is only when we turn to pray for some other person or need that our attention is suddenly dispersed, which means that it was not the thought of God, not the sense of his presence that was the cause of this concentration, but our human concern. It does not mean that human concern is of no importance, but it means that the thought of a friend can do more than the thought of God, which is a serious point.[1]

In a way, authentic prayer is always an unmasking. Man has to adore something: it may be money, status, career, fashion, law and order, establishment, revolution, or anything else. But one who truly adores God, thereby deposes all idols. Adoration thus becomes a liberating force. It is penetrating, unmasking all that is not God. It breaks down prejudices and leads to the truth. It also puts into place my own self. That is to say, prayer is an act of expropriation. Life is not merely a property of mine which I own; it is not given to me once and for all at the moment of my birth, but rather every day it is given anew until the very end. This expropriation is not alienation, however; it involves no denial of the essential meaning of human life.

Rather, it is an affirmation of the truth of my being. Prayer means that I go to the very Source from which everything derives its being. To pray means to assume a way of life which is receptive. I become not an owner, but a receiver. As soon as I start to control my life, taking everything into my own hands, I stop praying "Thy will be done." Here we touch the core of contemplation in action.

Perhaps we can express it in this image: to pray is to sit open-handed before God. He may take, he may give. My life is open for him. The gesture of the open hand denotes also that in prayer we do not achieve anything, that prayer is not an accomplishment. It is just letting oneself be loved by God, or more exactly, it is letting God be God (for God is love). Now in my work I can either maintain this same attitude of open-handed receptivity, or I can transform my work into a seizing; that is, I can use my activities to build up my self-image, to make myself important in my work, to assert myself in my actions. If this is the case, I have set up a fundamental opposition between the attitude of prayer and that of work, and my life is split asunder: contemplation and action have become antinomies; their oneness is gone. But I can also work in an attitude of prayer, making of my work a sincere service to God and to men, not seeking to build myself up, but again, as in prayer, giving and spending myself. It is in this kind of giving that one really receives: "Anyone who tries to preserve his life will lose it; and anyone who loses it will keep it safe" (Lk 17:33). Work done in this spirit will be humble and selfless. Now there is one attitude which pervades both contemplation and action; we have come to the root where the two are one. This "radical" unification stands for both authentic prayer and fruitful activity.

Prayer of this kind is not an escape, but a commitment. It is not merely saying, "Your will be done;" it is living it. Such activity is not self-appropriation, but unassuming service. It is letting God be God not only in our prayer but in our work. Prayer without action can be lazy, cheap. It is as though we said, "Lord, please help so that we won't have to do it." Action without prayer can be self-complacent, shallow, arbitrary. This may be one reason why St. Ignatius, who always taught, especially to his young men, that it was easy to find God in everything, laid at the same time great stress on mortification. Contemplation in action requires mortification both as its condition and as its fruit. Ignatius was genuinely concerned that people should not fool themselves in this, mistakenly accepting the false for the genuine. Contemplation in action is too precious an ideal to be squandered.

Five B

LIFE ROOTED IN PRAYER

A life rooted in prayer is a very simple life; in fact its very richness lies in its simplicity. Stripped of all that is non-essential, it boils down to a glad response made to the request of Jesus, "Remain in my love" (Jn 15:9).

— To live rooted in prayer is to live in the presence of the Father who is love; he is a love based on nothing, but he forms the basis of everything else, including our very existence.

— A life rooted in prayer is one in which we open ourselves to God's Word, which we contemplate in Christ "with unveiled faces" (2 Cor 3:18). We let that Word ring out in our hearts, and thus let the kingdom of God grow in us and through us.

— A life rooted in prayer makes it possible for us to be taken up into that conversation which the Father has with the Son and the Son with the Father, and which takes place in the Holy Spirit: "The Spirit too comes to help us in our weakness. For when we cannot choose words in order to pray properly, the Spirit himself expresses our plea in a way that could never be put into words, and God who knows everything in our hearts knows perfectly well what he means, and that the pleas of the saints expressed by the Spirit are according to the mind of God" (Rom 8:26-27).

It is thus by our life rooted in prayer that we become one with the Blessed Trinity and realize something of that salvation for which Jesus came into this world. And all this happens in faith, which is the first and the last word of all. It is always faith which Jesus asks: "Do you believe?" Faith does not imply that we do not make full use of our faculties, but it does mean that we use them in such a way that God can work in them and through them. At such times a certain experience of God in prayer may come over us—not extraordinary psychic phenomena nor very strong feelings of affection and emotion, nor superlatively clear intellectual insights. It is more simple and more quiet than that, less sensational, much more sober. In fact, the experience of God in prayer is for ninety-nine percent so lowly and unadorned that activity almost always seems more appealing and more pleasant. Moreover, the experience of God normally pre-supposes much preliminary, tedious effort. It is like a crust of dry bread. We are to feed on a humble, unobtrusive, persevering search for God with very little human satisfaction in the search. Nevertheless, in this pursuit we are willing to sacrifice everything else.

To be prayerful entails being attentive, waiting for God, interiorly emptying ourselves. To pray is not to hear oneself talk; it is rather to make oneself so still that God's Word can come through. Prayer is not the outpouring of the heart, a verbose expression of all its emotions. It is, rather, a persevering search for God and for the way to him, a search that is pursued whether the heart be full or empty. Prayer is by no means always spontaneous; it often requires a willed activity. It is an intimacy with the Invisible, a surrender, an abandonment, a willingness to do whatever he may ask, a marveling at his goodness, a growing symbiosis with his Word, a loneliness with and because of God, a deep and growing silence whose depth we long to explore.

Above all, prayer is a final commitment to God who is present, but whose presence is made known to us only in faith. Because of this faith we can persevere in our desire for communion with God whom we cannot locate, and then we can continue to live by that fullness we cannot grasp or even touch, and to let him truly be our life (Col 3:4). Thus, a person of prayer realizes in a very demanding way a fundamental aspect of God's kingdom on earth. In his priestly prayer Jesus asked: "May they all be one. Father, may they be one in us" (Jn 17:21). One who prays comes closest to the realization of this wish of Christ because such a person is one with the Father and the Son. In this way he builds up the people of God, which is the Church. That is why for our ecumenical efforts prayer is important. In spite of the divisions we encounter, we can find each other in God. On the contrary, a person who does not pray can be sure that he has lost what we have in common.

The person who dedicates his life to becoming ever more prayerful experiences within himself a strange paradox: he has found God in the certainty of his faith and, at the same time, he is seeking God in the darkness of his belief. He thanks God for having revealed himself, and yet he is begging God not to hide his face (Ps 27:9). God is at once very real for him, a Person with whom he communicates, but he is also like a wall—like a blank wall, as St. Thérèse explained so graphically. These paradoxes can be painful; they insure that the experiences of God normally are neither ecstatic nor exuberant, but rather, in a healthy way, disenchanting, denuding, humiliating. There are powerlessness and impotence involved, a continuous falling short of the ideal toward which we are reaching. We feel impelled to do more for God and we want to, but we cannot. Significantly, this falling short, however painful, is neither discouraging nor depressing since the basis of all prayer-life is the conviction that God is infinitely reliable, that he will never let us down no matter what we may do, that always he keeps loving us for what we are.

The wonder is, then, that in all this emptiness life continues its growth. There is a dryness, a dissatisfaction; yet these cannot lure us away to the more simple route of mere activity. In fact, the difficulties encountered in a life of prayer enable us to share in the fidelity of God. God is ever faithful to us, and we, therefore, in the darkness of our struggle remain faithful to him. It is this faithfulness which shows how real God is. Perhaps this is the heart of all apostolate, so that only a life rooted in prayer can be truly apostolic. In the first place, it is not the achievements that count; rather it is the *source* from which they flow that is really important. Our greatest service to our fellowmen (and our least appreciated one too) may possibly be the service of our prayer.

It is an essential task of the Church to teach us how to pray, for in this way only shall we ever be able to reform her structures and truly to renew her. It is only in prayer that we can reach beyond the system and touch the source. Prayer renders us a sign of God in spite of ourselves. No one prays in order to be a sign for others, of course—there are more rewarding ways in which to impress people! One who desires explicitly to make his life witness will always fail. Without wanting to be a witness, however, prayerful people are just that. I think the most genuine apostles are not much concerned with the meaningfulness of their lives; they merely give their lives away in faith and love for God. This truth has been verbalized in a letter from a Little Brother of Jesus:

The ideal of apostolic life or the ideal of contemplative life—every ideal has to be purified from everything that is not leading directly to God. I only want in an absolute and total way to make God's love the motive of all my actions and I want to be guided only by that love, by its demands and invitations. I want to remain faithful to these because I have been captured by that love. All that is not the love of God has no meaning for me...I can say that I have no interest in anything but that love of God which is in Christ Jesus. If God wants it so, my life will be useful through my example, my word, my action, my witnessing. If he wants it so, my life will be fruitful by my prayer, my sacrifices. The usefulness of my life is his concern, not mine. He arranges everything in such a way that my life will bear fruit. It would be indecent for me to worry about that.[1]

In this man I sense the core of a life lived entirely for God. In that core, contemplation and action are truly synthesized; the contemplative and the active are one.

In the last analysis, contemplation and action are both forms of an ardent desire truly to give one's life to God in whatever way he wants it. This desire transcends any concern about being up-to-date, of reaching fulfillment, of being meaningful to others. Not infrequently, prayer may almost palpably seem experienced as a waste of time. However, this is all to the good, for the waste of time is merely a symbol of a far deeper erosion—namely, the waste of self which will mean the ultimate and only way in which the soul can bear fruits that last. It is this fundamental attitude of contemplation, this willingness to be consumed, which must pervade our action also.

A life rooted in prayer seeks silence, but in the profound sense—an inner silence which means "no self-concern, no desire for attention." To be silent in this sense means to experience the quiet that comes when all forms of self-involvement are hushed and the soul can be truly still. Genuine prayer is not introspection. On the contrary, when prayer becomes self-centered, even if it be centered upon our noble and holy aspirations and plans, there is something seriously wrong. The focus of true prayer is not "I, me, or my;" hence the spotlight in prayer must not be turned on oneself (in the review *after* prayer it may), but away from oneself and on Christ. The time of prayer is the time for seeing only Jesus. To contemplate him is the most efficient way to improve oneself because then it is the Holy Spirit himself who will work in us the change he desires: "We with our unveiled faces reflecting like mirrors the brightness of the Lord, all grow brighter and brighter as we are turned into the image that we reflect; this is the work of the Lord who is Spirit" (2 Cor 3:18). By thus concentrating on God's glory as enfleshed in Jesus we experience a deeper transformation than any ascetic endeavor can achieve and we shall bear richer fruit than any we can produce by ourselves. This explains also why true contemplatives are good listeners. They are accustomed in prayer to direct their attention away from themselves; in a conversation then, they do the same almost naturally, focusing complete attention on the other.

While a life of prayer is an adventure that can fail in several ways, it can succeed, I think, in only one: through an ever more complete surrender to God. This surrender can grow in a special way during times of desolation because then, clearly, I am finding no satisfaction in it for myself. It is a pruning that must precede any complete abandonment to God, a guarantee of a more abundant harvest to come: "Every branch that does bear fruit he

70

prunes to make it bear even more" (Jn 15:2). In times of desolation the temptation will be strong to seek fulfillment in another way. Yet this sheer emptiness is an indispensable part of the prayer-life. Without a staunch fidelity to the practice of prayer in this dark desert, prayer itself might become selfish. It may be of some help at times such as these to remind ourselves that all men and women of prayer have gone through these experiences. Christ himself was not excluded: "My God, my God, why have you deserted me?" (Mt 27:46; Ps 22:1). This same anguish is found in many of the psalms:

> Let me say to God my Rock,
> 'Why do you forget me?
> Why must I walk
> so mournfully, oppressed by the enemy?' (Ps 42:9).

> Worn out with calling, my throat is hoarse,
> my eyes are strained looking for my God (Ps 69:3).

> But I am here, calling for your help,
> praying to you every morning:
> why do you reject me?
> Why do you hide your face from me? (Ps 88:13-14).

> If only I knew how to reach him,
>   or how to travel to his dwelling!. . .
> If I go eastward, he is not there;
>   or westward—still I cannot see him.
> If I seek him in the north, he is not to be found,
>   invisible still when I turn to the south (Job 23:3, 8-9).

In a poem that sings of a soul rejoicing to know God by faith alone, John of the Cross emphasizes his theme by the haunting refrain: "How well I know the fount that freely flows although 'tis night." The night may be dark, but I know in faith that the fount flows freely even though I cannot perceive it in any way. God is in a cloud where he cannot be seen. Do not run away. Stay. This is part of the rooting of a life in prayer. Now we are no longer in control. We no longer can arrange our life in such a way that we feel it is meaningful or fruitful. Instead, we know only a dreadful sense of wasting. This type of prayer stands for a way of life, a life that is given to God in the first place, but given to men also. This is becoming a contemplative in action. This is the transformation into an apostle, a transformation achieved not merely by our organizations and activities, but above all by what we are, by our whole selves.

It may be that the future of the active congregations in the Church today depends upon whether they will be contemplative enough. In our time of secularization, the only totally inexpendable mission of religious is that of being genuinely contemplative in their actions. Every other task can be taken over by others; even now, this transfer of responsibilities is in process. Also, it is incontestable that faithful perseverance in desolate prayer is a form of solidarity with modern man for whom God is often so distant and so vague. If we do not seek escape in lesser compensations now, but choose to remain close to our God whom we experience only in dark faith, we convey to the world not with words or with striking achievements, but with our whole selves the assurance that faith does make sense and that God is real and reliable even though he is invisible. Then contemplation has itself become apostolate.

Six

THE BARREN NO: REFUSING TO BE LOVED

Faith is the conviction that God loves us as we are. This is really the core of our faith, and the whole of scripture and all theology are just an elaboration of this. Prayer is our response to this love, basking in it, opening ourselves completely in order to be loved fully by God. And sin, on the contrary, is the screening off of self from this love. It is saying, whether explicitly or implicitly, consciously or subconsciously, "No, I don't need it" to the love which God is offering.

We are all free to refuse God's love. Precisely because God *is* love in its purest form, he leaves us at liberty, for real love never imposes itself. Possessiveness and pressure are impurities that degrade love and cannot be found in God. Respect is the heart of love, and where it is lacking, one can give a gift worth a million dollars but will do more harm than good because the gesture is condescending. If in a marriage husband and wife lose respect for each other, low tide is setting in. Because God has infinite respect for us, he allows us full freedom. He desires our love, no doubt; he solicits it. And even more, he wants his love to be accepted; he yearns to make our hearts his home. But he will never force us.

All sin is a form of self-exaltation, the attempt to be the author of one's own happiness rather than to receive this happiness from God. The effort to create this happiness for himself, an utterly impossible accomplishment for man, constitutes sin in its most basic form. Man cannot produce the deepest values in human life; they can only be received. It is God alone who can give ultimate fulfillment, complete peace, and if man tries to achieve these values by himself, he is doomed to fail. This attempt we call sin.

Strange as it may sound, there required a true *metanoia* before a man can allow himself to be loved by God. This is one of the most profound paradoxes of the human situation, for on the one hand everyone yearns for this love of God, and yet it requires a fundamental change of mentality before a man can let the love of God really flow into his life. There is something in us which shrinks from being receptive. We all have such a strong tendency to be autonomous, to control our own lives, and in so doing, to make ourselves happy. *Metanoia*, that word which scripture uses so often, means a deep, personal reorientation to God, a change in my priorities and values, in my actions and reactions; it is really an existential transformation reaching to the depth of my being. This *metanoia* is vital, for the man who does not let himself be loved by God makes of his life a sterile thing. Perhaps the Pharisee as portrayed in the gospel is the best example of a man who refuses to allow himself to be loved by God. In a way, we are all Pharisees.

Mark begins his gospel:

> After John [the Baptist] had been arrested, Jesus went into Galilee. There he proclaimed the Good News from God. 'The time has come' he said 'and the kingdom of God is close at hand. Repent, and believe the Good News' (Mk 1:14-15).

The sequence is explicit: faith presupposes repentance: "Repent, and believe the Good News." Before we can accept this tremendous gift of the Good News, we have to change, for without this transformation our life will remain sterile. This is a constant thought in scripture: the sterility which results from closing oneself to God's love. One of the most poignant expressions of this tragic resistance of man to God's invitation is found in the song of the vineyard:

> What could I have done for my vineyard
> that I have not done?
> I expected it to yield grapes.
> Why did it yield sour grapes instead? (Is 5:4)

This is an image of the man who does not open himself to God's lavish care. The fruits of his life, as a consequence, will be sour, yielding no good wine, but only acid. Christ had the same message for us: "It is to the glory of my Father that you should bear much fruit, and then you will be my disciples" (Jn 15:8). Indeed, God wants us to be fruitful, wants our lives to be meaningful. In no other way can we be disciples of Christ.

Sin can be considered on two levels, one of which is the more obvious and its effects more immediately seen. On this concrete level we understand those actions which are more tangible: slandering, cheating, stealing, and the like. These concrete sins, however, are only the results of that deeper level, which is sin as the screening off of oneself from the action of God. On the concrete level we can say that all sins are attempts to fill up a gap in our lives; on the deeper level, we can understand that the gap need not be there at all. God is great enough to fill my heart, and to fill it to the brim. On this level we can say men are like plants which can decide for themselves whether or not they will turn towards the sun. Actually, the plant will always turn towards the sun because without sunlight it can have no growth. But *we* can decide whether we will turn towards the sun to receive its light or whether we will turn away from it, becoming sterile in doing so.

We would do well to consider sin not just as a moral problem—that would be the concrete sins—but as a more basic disorientation: the fettering of a person to that which exists so that he is not really open to the beyond. When love does not reach the deepest core of my heart, the outside world becomes a threat. Situations and the people around me do not give me sufficient scope. I find that they oppress me, threatening me not because they are bad in themselves, but because deep in my own heart there is something wrong. It is here that I find the root of evil. Since the world becomes a threat to me, I tend to be defensive and, perhaps, even aggressive, and in the consequent struggle I commit many faults. These are the concrete sins.

Scripture has many examples, at once beautiful and profound, of the disastrous effects of not letting God be God in our lives. When I make this great refusal, at the same time I ruin my own existence. This makes sense since God is the deepest Ground of my being. Sin is self-destruction: "It is death to limit oneself to what is unspiritual; life and peace can only come with concern for the spiritual" (Rom 8:6). Expressions such as "I do not understand myself," "I feel like a fraud, a phony," "If only they knew. . ." etc., show how guilt tears us apart, causes a split in our personality. "I cannot understand my own behavior. I fail to carry out the things I want to do, and I find myself doing the very things I hate. . . .instead of doing the good things I want to do, I carry out the sinful things I do not want" (Rom 7:15, 19). There comes about a certain disintegration of my personality in which I am trapped, and alienated from God, I am also estranged from myself. It is obvious that in this way I inflict great harm not only on myself, but also on my relations with others. The tower of Babel, described in an early chapter of Genesis, is a good example of this kind of social disruption (Gen 11). It relates the story of a people who set out to build a tower reaching to heaven which will make a name for them. The tower reaching into heaven means that they will be on the same level as God, equal with him. They no longer have to be receptive because of their new footing. They do not have to receive their name from God who first spoke it; now they make their own name. This is what is meant by refusing to let God be God in their life. The result, as described in scripture, was chaos; the people could no longer communicate with one another. Such an eventuality may seem, at first, to make no sense, but at closer scrutiny it does because there is a profound connection between our relations with each other and our relations with God. This is exactly the point of the story. When our relations with God are disturbed, the relations of man with man will likewise be disjointed. When God is excluded from my life, then I lose my name, my identity. Then I can no longer be addressed by others because I no longer have that which makes me truly a person. I can no longer relate authentically to others; hence, community is torn apart and divisions appear: *ubi peccata, ibi schismata*, where there are sins there will also be cracks.

The story of Babel is a forceful example of this disruption of natural harmony, but the same disorder resulting from sin had already been told in the account of Adam's sin in Paradise (Gen 3). Basically, the fall of Adam has the same point as the building of the tower. Adam and Eve eat from the fruit of the tree in order to obtain knowledge of good and evil. Knowledge here has the implication of "creative knowledge" whereby I can decide for myself what I call good and what I call bad. I no longer have to listen; I can run my own life. The temptation of the serpent is explicit: "God knows in fact that on the day you eat it your eyes will be opened and you will be like gods, knowing good and evil" (Gen 3:5). For Adam and Eve the temptation was to become their own God—and the result was that after they had eaten, the eyes of both were opened. . .and they realized that they were naked. Until this moment they had merely been unclothed, and they could relate to each other without shame or tension. As soon as their relation with God is disturbed, however, the relation between themselves is also disturbed. Now they are ashamed of each other and they try to hide. Once men are cut off from God they drift apart from one another; they become alienated and estranged. A whole art of hiding techniques is developed, in which much energy is expended. The straightforward lie is, of course, just as primitive and unbecoming a cover as the loin-cloth of fig-leaves. But more sophisticated evasions are quite acceptable and subconscious compensations are common. Some illusions might even be defended by falling ill, if need be. Then there is also the camouflage of taking over the color of one's surroundings, so that we may come up to the expectations of those around and win their approval, often at the expense of our own conscience.

Such subterfuges are sufficiently harmful in themselves, but in their wake inevitably a more fundamental rift appears, as we see in the subsequent actions of Adam and Eve. Overwhelmed by shame and anxiety, each seeks to evade responsibility and instead of acknowledging personal wrong-doing tries to hold another guilty for the wrong he has done. Adam casts the guilt on Eve: "It was the woman you put with me; she gave me the fruit, and I ate it." In the same way Eve accuses the serpent: "The serpent tempted me and I ate." This failure in personal integrity is one of the immediate consequences of sin.

The disorder of sin travels quickly. Chapter 3 of Genesis narrates the first sin; Chapter 4 tells of the first murder, and the subsequent story of mankind shows how quickly the ravages of sin destroy the relations of men. After murder in natural sequence there follow the thoughts of revenge, as expressed in the sword-song of Lamech:

> Lamech said to his wives:
> 'Adah and Zillah, hear my voice,
> Lamech's wives, listen to what I say:
> I killed a man for wounding me,
> a boy for striking me.
> Sevenfold vengeance is taken for Cain,
> but seventy-sevenfold for Lamech (Gen 4:23-24).

The spirit of vengeance comes over man; he turns resentful and bitter, and all this because men wanted to be their own gods.

To describe these ravages of sin scripture also uses the image of the hardening of the heart; man becomes calloused, stubborn. Enclosed in his own self, he cannot get out nor relate to others. Scripture says of Pharaoh that his heart was hardened and stubborn (Ex 10:20). This alienation from his fellowmen is explained a few chapters earlier when we see how Pharaoh explicitly cuts himself off from God: "Who is Yahweh," Pharaoh replied, "that I should listen to him and let Israel go? I know nothing of Yahweh..." (Ex 5:2). When we refuse to know Yahweh we build a wall around our heart and eventually we get trapped in our own bunker. In order to relate to each other we need God. When deep within my own heart I know myself loved, then I can open myself to others without being afraid. But if in my heart there is only coldness or lonesomeness, other people then become threatening. I may be able to relate to them superficially, but I cannot do so in a truly personal way.

I remember a novel about a nun who after twenty years of nursing in which she had made quite a career in her profession came to the dismaying discovery that she had never really dedicated herself to others. The people she had wanted to help were only projections and prolongations of herself. She had never truly resigned from herself, nor had she lost herself in another. Now she discovered how instead of helping people for twenty years, she had really been using the sick to forge her own career. What she had been calling service of the sick had really been service of herself. This is possible, of course; in my work I can focus on serving others—as I can and should—but it is also possible to use my "service" to build my own tower, to make a name for myself. Then I have used others for my own glorification or fulfillment. The sister had discovered that she was ensnared in her own self, that she could not really love the other person as other, but only as useful for herself. This is a basic aspect of sin; it precludes wholesome and authentic relations with other persons even though I may strive to hide this failure behind a mask that prevents the truth from showing through. There are many such masks available. I can, for example, wear a mask of cynical attitudes, of acrid remarks. In this way I keep everyone at a distance; no one will come near me because he dreads my sharp tongue. Thus I cover my inability to relate deeply with others. Or I can hide myself behind a continuous stream of arguing and endless discussions. By keeping the conversation on the discussion-level I make sure that no deeper contact is ever attempted. Or, for another mask I can retreat behind a facade of busyness. No one can approach me, intrude upon my real self because I am so extremely occupied. Behind this busyness I can hide my loneliness.

Sin treats other persons as if they were things. Rather than relate to them as persons, I use them in my own life as commodities. Perhaps the most extreme examples of reducing persons to things occur in wars, where troops and even civilians are reduced to "human material." What happened at My Lai, what happened at the Munich Olympics, what happened in Nazi concentration camps, what happened in the Spanish Civil War and in so many other wars show the defilement possible for human nature. These are extreme examples of disregard for one's fellow-men, but the same harshness can be seen in many lesser instances. We have all encountered at some time parents who in their love for their children can be too possessive. The father of a family who had wanted to become a doctor but who for any number of reasons had been unable to do so, may go to any lengths and pay any price to provide for his son the opportunity he himself had missed even though the boy may not want to be a doctor, but may have set his heart on another profession. If one were to tell the father that his insistence is really a lack of love, he would be deeply grieved. And yet, it is true. Such a parent, even while protesting love for his child, is not giving the boy a chance to be himself. What is really selfishness can so readily masquerade as love!

The mature Christian of today should leave aside all petty concern about lesser sins, transgressions of rules for children. His concern should be to examine himself on a much deeper level in order to discover what lack of love there may be in his heart. This lack of love can even be institutionalized, thus effecting a dangerous depersonalization by perpetuating structures which, in a sense, exact a kind of anonymity on the part of their members, who dehumanize both themselves and others in the process. The real evil is that in such deformed structures people cannot really be loved. They are an example of egoism objectified.

Every sin inflicts harm on my neighbor. When the sin is a concrete one—theft or calumny—I can see the harm quite readily, but hurt is inflicted also where the damage is not so obvious. Even that sin which is committed within the privacy of my heart does harm to others. François Mauriac says truly: "The day I no longer burn with love, many others will die of the cold." We are responsible for each other. He who commits evil denies the other person the blessing of a good man. There is a kind of hypocrisy in all sin, for this evil done to my fellow-man is so easily hidden. For religious this matter raises serious questions which we must face honestly. As religious we are dedicated to God, and yet does God really fill our lives? If he does, why is there so much sensitivity for our own honor? Why so much ambition, so much selfishness? Why is there such a lack of real poverty? Why so little concern about the terrible needs of large populations throughout the world? Are not these signs that God is not real enough in our lives? The evil is compounded also by the ever-present danger of scandal, which is a terrible thing in the eyes of Christ:

> But anyone who is an obstacle to bring down one of these little ones who have faith in me would be better drowned in the depths of the sea with a great millstone round his neck (Mt 18:6).

We have to help each other by making it easier to believe and hope and love. Our failure is all the greater if instead we become a hindrance to faith for others. Christ had harsh things to say to the Pharisees because they turned people aside from the kingdom of heaven:

> Alas, for you, scribes and Pharisees, you hypocrites! You who shut up the kingdom of heaven in men's faces, neither going in yourselves nor allowing others to go in who want to. Alas for you, scribes and Pharisees, you hypocrites! You who travel over sea and land to make a single proselyte, and when you have him you make him twice as fit for hell as you are (Mt 23:13-15).

In the same way, our deep core sin, not letting ourselves be loved by God, can do tremendous harm to others. We may live the gospel in such a way that it does not appeal to people; it is too ordinary, too mediocre to arouse their enthusiasm or their interest. We may distort the picture of God which they have in their hearts. But to do this is to fail seriously in our responsibility for each other. The point is always the same: when I let God be God in my life, then my life will be fruitful for all those for whom I bear responsibility, and in the design of God this means everyone, for I am responsible for all the people with whom I deal.

Seven

SALVATION TO THIS HOUSE

At first glance the situation seems ludicrous. Here we have Zacchaeus, an important man in that little border town of Jericho, an official high in the ranks of the internal revenue service, a wealthy man—and we find him perched in a tree, looking down in curiosity upon the crowd which thronged about a young rabbi from Nazareth! Outwardly, the picture does not seem to promise much in the way of spiritual sustenance. And yet in the encounter of Christ with Zacchaeus we find all the elements of the mission of Jesus, the savior, the one who has come to seek out and to save those who have been lost (Lk 19:1-10).

It was an unusual position for a man of Zacchaeus's rank, it is true, but that did not seem to bother him. He showed no inhibitions; he had only one thing on his mind: to see for himself what kind of man this Jesus really was. From several of his colleagues who had talked with the rabbi he had heard reports that had puzzled but intrigued him. Indeed, the very fact that Jesus would receive a tax collector was in itself extraordinary. A normal rabbi would never have done so, for tax collectors were looked upon as traitors, as evil men with whom one did not associate. If he did speak with tax collectors, this rabbi from Nazareth must be different, and Zacchaeus had to see him, for he was experiencing within himself a deep longing to talk with a spiritual man.

CALLED BY NAME

There was something wrong, something troubling Zacchaeus. It was not yet fully clear even in his own mind just what the problem was, but he had to do something. He would first merely look, would see what Jesus was like. Then if he found him approachable, he might perhaps go and have a talk with him, and if all went well during that conversation he might have the courage to discuss with this man his own deep qualms. For Zacchaeus was a seriously troubled man. The unanimous contempt of the whole town for tax collectors, the way in which he and his colleagues were looked down upon by their countrymen—all this was bad enough, but after all, it was only exterior, a skin-deep difficulty although after a while even this could become worrisome. But the real problem was an inner one: Zacchaeus was not at ease in his own conscience. Deep within, he knew himself for what he truly was: an extortioner, a man so greedy for ever more and more money that he did not hesitate even to the point of cruelty. Zacchaeus knew that he should not do these things; often he had determined to change his way of life. But his good resolutions never lasted long. He would remain honorable for a few days, then invariably he would stumble and find himself once again in the familiar rut.

To understand the situation of Zacchaeus we need to know how the Romans operated in their conquered territories. Having occupied almost the whole of the known world, the Romans found themselves faced with the problem of collecting tribute from their subject peoples. Astute administrators that they were, they understood that the task of collecting taxes, always an unpopular item, could best be handled by the inhabitants of the conquered territories themselves. As Romans they could never succeed, for always they were recognized as the enemy, and floundering in a swamp of determined opposition, they would find themselves entangled in a tacit but stubborn passive resistance. To solve the problem most lucratively and with least difficulty, the Romans had divided their occupied territories into regions, in each of which local citizens could rent or lease a section. For a fixed annual fee these men became the tax collectors, for whom any money collected over and above their rental fee was clear profit. The system proved simple for the Romans; instead of a hostile population, they had to deal only with those men who were willing to perform the unpopular task of collecting the money. It was an efficient system too, for the Romans could be sure that the tax collectors would get every last penny out of their areas; such industry was to their advantage.

This then is Zacchaeus' position. Because he works for the occupying forces, he is considered a traitor by his countrymen. Because he makes himself rich at the expense of his own, he is hated. Were it up to him, he would probably prefer a different system, but when he must make a choice between himself and others, invariably he chooses self. He is the victim of a structure and a system which he has not willed. At the same time he is an accomplice in the evil since the whole system can work only because there are willing tax collectors. If all of them were to refuse to cooperate, the system would collapse. But the Romans knew that they would never do this. Conceivably, one might have the strength to fight the system, but never all.

Zacchaeus is caught in a system which at the same time, paradoxically, he is helping to perpetuate. In him we see an alarming example of how egoism can be objectified in social structures. Individual sinfulness can be translated into a system operating in society. In this way it becomes hardened in institutions, at once impersonal and depersonalized, which eventually escape our direct control. It becomes tyrannical power, dehumanizing both the victims and the exploiters, probably the latter even more than the former. Caught up in the system, Zacchaeus is at once the victim and the sustainer, the oppressed and the oppressor, the instigator as well as the object of injustice embodied in a powerful system. It is hard to figure out in how far he is oppressor and in how far he is oppressed. The two intermingle in the system and cannot be separated. Zacchaeus finds himself enmeshed in this structure, this power, and it is Jesus who frees him from his captivity. Jesus—*savior*, *salvator*: the one who makes people free.

At first Zacchaeus merely wants to see what Jesus looks like, what kind of man he is. But the tax collector is too short; he cannot see for the crowd. Here we find another likeness with our own situation. It can indeed be the crowd which prevents us from seeing Jesus. We must climb above the crowd in order to see Jesus, but take care—to climb above the crowd is dangerous! The crowd does not take too kindly to this kind of thing. It is the scorn of our peers more than anything else which hinders us in our search for God. We are afraid of what others may say. This fear of ridicule paralyzes more effectively than would a head-on attack or an outspoken, harsh criticism. How much good is left undone because of our fear of the opinions of others! We are immobilized by the thought: what will others say? The irony of all this is that the opinions we fear most are not those of people we really respect, yet these same persons influence our lives more than we want to admit. This enervating fear of our peers can create an appalling mediocrity.[1] Henri Nouwen has

quoted David Riesman, the Harvard psychologist, who in
his article on American universities has some penetrating
comments on this subject which are as applicable to
religious life as to the campus: "As adult authority
disintegrates, the young are more and more the captives of
each other...When adult control disappears, the young's
control of each other intensifies." This observation leads
Nouwen to reflect:

> Instead of the father, the peer becomes the standard. Many
> young people who are completely unimpressed by the de-
> mands, expectations, and complaints of the big bosses of the
> adult world, show a scrupulous sensitivity to what their peers
> feel, think, and say about them. . . .Many young people may
> even become enslaved by the tyranny of their peers. While
> appearing indifferent, casual, and even dirty to their elders,
> their indifference is often carefully calculated, their casualness
> studied in the mirror, and their dirty appearance based on a
> detailed imitation of their friends.[2]

The tyranny of our peers! We must climb above it if
we wish to see who Jesus really is. Zacchaeus had the
courage to climb above the crowd even though we may be
sure they laughed at him, a senior tax collector, in this
ridiculous position. But at the time Zacchaeus did not care
because all he wanted was to catch a glimpse of Jesus.
Once he found himself in the tree, however, the unexpect-
ed began. Jesus, the rabbi whom he did not know, acted as
if he had known Zacchaeus for a long time, as if they had
been good friends. And indeed Zacchaeus *was* his friend
because it was for people like him that Jesus had come:
"...indeed I did not come to call the virtuous, but
sinners" (Mt 9:13). Since Zacchaeus was a sinner, he was

one whom Christ was seeking. In the gospels we see an interesting relationship between Christ and sinners. His name, expressive of his whole mission, is Jesus: "...because he is the one who is to save his people from their sins" (Mt 1:21). And here in the tree was a man to be saved. It is revealing to see how Jesus acts with the people he serves. The sick who are brought to him he cures; but for sinners he goes out of his way, and as in this instance he takes the initiative. He addressed the troubled man: "Zacchaeus, come down. Hurry, because I must stay at your house today." Come down, that is the first thing to do. We must have our two feet on earth; otherwise Jesus cannot deal with us.

Then Jesus and Zacchaeus walked together through the streets of Jericho, and the stunned tax collector could scarcely believe what was happening. Indeed, this rabbi was different. He might not have a degree, but he was truly a *rabbi*. He seemed untouched by the carping of the crowds who pressed around, complaining that he was going to the home of a sinner. He was not looking around anxiously, fearing what people might say. He was unafraid of their remarks. He was going to the home of Zacchaeus because this man was a good friend of his—that was all.

Once in the house, Jesus's sensitive thoughtfulness continued. He did not talk to Zacchaeus like a Dutch uncle. He merely showed unbounded trust and love. "The kindness and love of God our savior for mankind were revealed" (Tit 3:4). This was something Zacchaeus had not experienced for many years, kindness, love—not condemnation or pressure, just love. This was an experience so unusual for Zacchaeus that something was bound to happen within him. And suddenly the change occurred! So long as he found himself under pressure, he could never change; as soon as that pressure was removed and acceptance had taken its place, the change was possible. Once in his home, Zacchaeus had to speak, and he burst out: "Look, sir, I am going to give half my property to the poor, and if I have cheated anybody I will pay him back four times the amount." There are some words people utter routinely, words lacking buoyancy and force, but these words of Zacchaeus rushed out with tremendous power. They were not normal, ordinary words; they were an oath, spoken in the presence of God, welling up from a great depth because the conversion they signify had been repressed for so long. That is why they were so forceful. And Zacchaeus knew they were an irrevocable break with the past. The die was cast. What he had tried half-heartedly so many times had happened all at once here in his encounter with Jesus. He had learned what we all must learn: once we admit the Lord behind the facade and into our heart, we can be sure something is going to change. In an instant Zacchaeus broke with his money, with his position, with all he had clung to. True, he had been a prisoner of the Roman system, but he could be imprisoned only because he had clung to his money. Once this attachment was broken he was no longer bound; he had become a free man.

"I am going to give half my property to the poor, and if I have cheated anybody I will pay him back four times the amount." We might be tempted to be critical of Zacchaeus. He is giving only half; is this conversion? Why not all? Half a restoration seems merely a prelude to conversion. Then too Zacchaeus is still running the show himself; he is still the principal agent; *he* is going to do these things. He seems not to realize that conversion is something God works in us. In the previous chapter Luke had told of the publican who prayed: "God, be merciful to me, a sinner" (18:14). Surely, this seems a truer conversion, the response of a man who knows that we depend entirely on God's mercy. Then too, Zacchaeus seems to consider sin much too superficially. He seems to think it is a matter merely of finances, a wrong that can be righted by four-fold restitution. This is not true, of course, for Zacchaeus's evil is on a deeper level. He has grieved people, hurt them, has sown hard feelings among them, possibly even has driven them to despair. These are evils which cannot be cured by money. There is more to conversion than Zacchaeus has realized.

It may be true that he has not yet understood the full evil of his ways, but such realization is not necessary for conversion. Zacchaeus yearns for a new life, and it is this longing which Jesus hears and encourages. He speaks reassuringly to the man who is groping towards forgiveness: "Today salvation has come to this house, because this man too is a son of Abraham, for the Son of Man has come to seek out and save what was lost." Jesus accepts what Zacchaeus offers. Not turned aside by the wrong in what is said, he is on the lookout for the right. And he has found enough of this in the words of Zacchaeus to encourage him. God is at work in this man; salvation has come to this house. Zacchaeus has experienced a new birth, and God wants only to forgive and to celebrate the new life that is awakening.

God's forgiveness—a mystery of love! God forgives in so many ways, forgives even before we ask. The problem of forgiveness is not on God's side, but on ours. God forgives readily, with infinite finesse, and even while we are still committing sin, he is already forgiving. But it is we who are remiss. The question really is: how can *we* absorb this forgiveness of God? How can we rid ourselves of guilt? It is the sense of guilt which proves our greatest pitfall. There are many whose lives are crushed under a weight of guilt. They play games, of course, so that others may not know their real sorrow, but if once we get to know them, we understand better their true plight. They are bound fast, cannot unfold, cannot really live their ideals because of the darkness which overshadows them. Haunted by this sense of unworthiness, they cannot convince themselves that they truly belong among God's friends, and the life to which in the depths of their souls they aspire seems ever more unattainable. This conviction of unworthiness ends by ruining their lives, eroding their energy, wholly ener-vating them so that any movement out of the morass seems hopeless. For such persons—and at some time all of us experience this ebb-tide of hope—the agonizing question becomes: How can I be rid of guilt? How can I absorb with my whole heart the assurance of God's forgiveness?

It is here that the mercy of God manifests itself, for the answer is prompt and simple: Forgiveness is always there. It is when I acknowledge failure and guilt that the forgiveness becomes mine. God forgives in many ways, it is true, promptly, completely, but he has given the sacrament of confession as the means *par excellence* by which we attain not only the reality of forgiveness, but the true, interior realization of pardon and of peace which are at once the fruits and the proof of God's forgiveness. The sacrament is the official channel given by God in which his forgiveness reaches us more intensely and most explicitly. In the sacrament I confess my guilt, verbalizing the wrong I have done, telling it to another, and I receive the absolution spoken aloud by one who has received this power. This is the only ultimate, human way in which I can expressly get rid of my guilt and experience God's forgiveness.

In Latin the word *confessio* has a double meaning, *viz.* to praise God (as in the *Confessions of St. Augustine*) and to express one's sins in the sacrament. There is a close link between these two meanings of the word. The gospel says several times that no one can forgive sins but God alone. When I receive the sacrament of penance, therefore, I am letting myself be forgiven; but since only God can do this for me, I am, so to speak, offering God a chance to work in me an eminently and exclusively divine effect. In other, briefer words, I let God be God. That is also *confessio,* praising him.

This is what Zacchaeus experienced. He met God, encountered him in the human person of Jesus, and found that he could express his guilt. Then when he had heard the words of pardon, he found that he could truly absorb this overwhelming forgiveness, could really experience a new start in his life. Christ had told Nicodemus that a man must be born again (Jn 3:1-8). At this moment Zacchaeus was experiencing rebirth, for grace was happening here. Later, he would sound the true depths of his guilt. Often it is only in expiating our sins that we learn how terrible they really are. In his *Pensées* Pascal wrote: You will get to know the depth of your guilt only to the degree in which you expiate it. This makes sense. When I set about repairing the havoc, then I learn how much damage has been done. Zacchaeus too will discover all this later. When he comes to the people with four times the amount he has cheated them of, he will find that some will not want the money. Embittered, they will cast it back in his face, and he will be amazed. It is only then that he will find out how people have been led even to despair by his acts.

Realization will come, but that will be later. Right now, he need not fear. The Lord has helped him to make a new start; the Lord will help him to continue, to bring all to a good end. There is still work to be done, but now things will be different, for the whole mentality of the man has been changed by Christ. How did this come about? It was simple: Christ had not condemned him, but had accepted him as he was. That is the miracle of the love and kindness of God which Zacchaeus had experienced. Now there is a new birth.

There is a final reflection on the situation of Zacchaeus in his tree. Zacchaeus was short; he had to climb the tree. If he had not been short, would he ever have climbed? And if he had not climbed, would all this have happened?

Eight

GOD WITH US

Revelation, in a sense, is an invitation into the mystery of God, given that we may know not with merely intellectual enlightenment, but with that response of our whole being which represents profound personal affirmation. It is a glimpse into the activity of God, ever at work in his universe, ever seeking the happiness and deep peace for men which from the beginning he had envisaged, and yet, in respect for the awesome mystery of man's freedom, ever waiting for man to accept the call and freely to say yes to the gift. This interplay of God's initiative and man's response, constituting the basis of Christian life, is found in each mystery of Christ, but perhaps nowhere more vividly than in the incarnation. To contemplate this mystery prayerfully is to seek for a realization with my heart of who Christ really is, to strive for that knowledge which comes only from a close personal relationship with him. A husband gets to know his wife in the first place not by studying a book on feminine psychology, but by living with her, sharing with her the joys and aspirations and pains of their life together. In this way he learns what makes her unique, a special person, the one he truly loves. This is the kind of knowledge of Christ which I am seeking—not merely a general collection of platitudes, but a deep, wholly personal understanding of his personality so that I may love him, may imitate him, may become, as it were, another Christ, a second humanity to help others understand better who Christ is and why he has come.

CALLED BY NAME

Everything about the incarnation bespeaks the initiative of God. It is God who knows and examines each man on earth with the keen concern of a vigilant shepherd looking after his flock and with the loving care of a father to whom all life is precious. No human misery escapes his attention. And of this misery there is plenty! He sees so much suffering in the world, so much anguish in the hearts of men. Where we comprehend only a fraction of it, he perceives the whole. None of this pain is God's desire, for it is his glory that man should prosper exteriorly and interiorly. The worst suffering of all may well be the feeling of guilt. Some of this is neurotic and inauthentic, and has to be cured. But some of it is genuine, and for this there is no natural cure. Here only forgiveness can restore wholeness. And who but God alone can forgive sins? God also offered to take away by himself that greatest misery of all—guilt—by proclaiming his eagerness to forgive. Above all, God wanted man to realize that in spite of his shortcomings and sins, he was still loved. This was the unvarying content of what the prophets had to say, each in his own style—some brilliant, some rather clumsy, but all bearing the same inspired communication. They had something more in common, though, namely that none of them succeeded in their mission with lasting effect.

Then God appoints a time to be the "fullness of time" (Gal 4:4) in which he speaks to us through his Son. "He had still someone left: his beloved son. He sent him to them last of all" (Mk 12:6). While the manner of the Son's coming was wholly different, the message which he conveyed was in line with what the prophets had always preached. Jesus himself sums up the purpose of his coming into the world in the pregnant statement: "I was born for this, I came into the world for this, to bear witness to the

98

truth" (Jn 18:37), where truth means the reliability of God's love. In his conversation by night with Nicodemus Jesus makes the same point at greater length:

> Yes, God loved the world so much
> that he gave his only Son,
> so that everyone who believes in him may not be lost,
> but may have eternal life.
> For God sent his Son into the world
> not to condemn the world,
> but so that through him the world might be saved
>   (Jn 3:16-17).

It is the assurance of salvation which Christ brings, but this time there is so much more than the message, for he is the incarnation of the Word, which is God, and of the radiant light of God's glory. He is the Son of God become one of us so as to give his message not in words, but in a way of life. Jesus can accomplish this way, can even begin it only by emptying himself. *Kenosis* is the first step in his mission and the key-note for his life.

> His state was divine,
> yet he did not cling
> to his equality with God
> but emptied himself
> to assume the condition of a slave,
> and became as men are;
> and being as all men are,
> he was humbler yet,
> even to accepting death,
> death on a cross (Phil 2:6-8).

The whole of his life was a carrying out of the initial

self-emptying. By means of his stripping, he became our brother; consequently, the world has changed, that world which he had created in a wonderful way and has re-created in a yet more wonderful way. Now indeed we can sing the *felix culpa* of Easter night: happy guilt that has given us such a redeemer and has brought God to such a point that he sent his own Son among us so that we might share his life even as he has willed to share ours.

But is God going to carry out this work of leading his people back to him and of renewing his covenant by himself? No, God wants to share with men this work of redemption. But whom will he choose? Here once again we see God's initiative in moving forward his plans for man's redemption, and the consistent trend of the *kenosis* in realizing salvation. With the whole vast Roman Empire extending before him, that culmination of man's achievement in the ancient world, God chose not the busy centers of man's industry or art, politics or learning, but one remote and isolated corner of the Empire, the occupied territory of Palestine. The Roman masters did not think much of this territory; they dismissed it as the most troublesome part of their whole Empire. Nor did they think highly of the Jews themselves, whom Tacitus was to describe as "a most contemptible mob of slaves" and "a most repellant people." Yet that nation is God's choice. Nor does the enigma of his selection stop here. For in the country of Palestine it was the province of Galilee that he chose, the most backward, most despised of the country, and in Galilee it was the village of Nazareth which he singled out, a village without history, so obscure that its name does not occur in the Old Testament. In all this we see the *kenosis* of Philippians 2: the incarnation is the mystery of the lowest place.

God with Us

How is God going to accomplish this mission—by imposing something? No, force and pressure are foreign to God; he comes with an invitation, a request, and then he leaves us free to respond. God's respect for the freedom of his creature is total. Even for such a sublime role as mother of the incarnate God the chosen young girl of Nazareth will be left to respond as she wishes. The vignette of the annunciation (Lk 1:26-38) is a perfect presentation of God's role and man's response in the mystery of the incarnation and in the life of each of us.

It begins with a little dialogue between the angel of God and Mary of Nazareth. The angel takes the initiative; Mary responds. This is always the format: God first presents his grace, and we are free to say yes or no. In the little home of Nazareth this dialogue had three movements. The angel began: "Rejoice, so highly favored! The Lord is with you." In a way, God says this to each of us because we are truly highly favored, first by the very fact that we exist since in itself this means that the immense love of God has called us into being. Then, we are favored in that we have been summoned for a greater purpose, entrusted with a special vocation, for this indicates that God is caring for us, inviting us into himself. Mary's reaction is utterly sincere: she is deeply disturbed by the words and asks herself what this greeting could mean. Her reaction is not so much in words, but in the puzzlement which comes over her at the angel's words. If we realize how much we mean to God by our existence, by our vocation, we too become speechless. The silence which follows upon fullness, upon being overwhelmed, may also be a need for inner stillness in order that we may let the reality dawn upon us and that we may be imbued by the joy of knowing that we are so highly favored. Because the

101

joy which God gives is never superficial, it does not find entrance readily; we have to open ourselves completely, in silence, to embrace this joy. Thus Mary's silence at the first words of the angel was an eloquent response of wonder.

The angel again takes the initiative, describing for Mary her call, her mission:

> Mary, do not be afraid; you have won God's favor. Listen! You are to conceive and bear a son, and you must name him Jesus. He will be great and will be called Son of the Most High. The Lord God will give him the throne of his ancestor David; he will rule over the House of Jacob for ever and his reign will have no end.

The angel here sums up the prophecies of many generations and expands them to the full extent of their promise. In Mary's unhampered openness to the action of God the partial and limited attempts of the prophets of the past can be brought to full completion. Through her God can speak his Word in its divine fullness. Mary the immaculate is wholly pure and unselfish, and therefore transparent to the divine without sifting anything from its infinite plenitude, so that through her the Son of the Most High can enter the world. Here in the little house of Nazareth we see the beginning of that work and note that Mary's part too begins with a *kenosis*: she does not expect to accomplish the work by herself. She asks the angel: "But how can this come about, since I am a virgin?" Unlike the question of Zechariah, which was one of doubt, Mary's question was one of openness, seriousness, an effort to enter more fully into the mission which the angel was communicating. Zechariah's doubt led to muteness, to a closing off of the dialogue. Mary's question led deeper into the mystery that God was opening to her that day.

God with Us

Again the angel spoke: "The Holy Spirit will come upon you, and the power of the Most High will cover you with its shadow. And so the child will be holy and will be called Son of God." The message is awe-inspiring for ears trained in the holy scriptures. To be covered with the shadow evokes the images of the power of the Most High, of the presence of Yahweh himself. The Ark of the Covenant was covered with the shadow. Now Mary's body will be the ark of the covenant. God will accomplish in her what is impossible for man. When we look on ourselves, we too see nothing but limitations, and the mission entrusted to us seems beyond our capacity, too heavy for our strength. All this, of course, is true in one way: the gospel is utterly impossible; none of us can follow Christ completely or meet his demands fully. But the words of the angel to Mary are likewise true for us: nothing is beyond the power of God. On this basis we can build; we no longer have to carry the burden by ourselves. We can trust in the Lord. It was on this foundation and on no other that Mary spoke her *fiat*: "I am the handmaid of the Lord, let what you have said be done to me."

The initiation of the mystery of God-made-man can thus be summarized in the three stages of this dialogue: God approaches; man hesitates. God proposes; man questions. God acts; man ventures. This sets the basic pattern of our dialogue with God. Mary surrenders wholly in her *fiat*, and the result is that she is filled with fruitfulness, the fruitfulness of the Holy Spirit himself, a fruitfulness beyond any human power or strength. God becomes incarnate in her womb. With Mary I can pray her Magnificat: He who is mighty has done great things for me. I can believe that God can use me too since he elects so often to use weak instruments, if these are willing to serve, to respond with a humble *fiat.* Only in a "yes" to God can my life really be fruitful and build the kingdom of God.

In Mary's "yes" the Son of God became one of us and shared our life. He has experienced with body and soul, heart and mind, what it means to be human. He knows what it means to have a body, to be caught within the limitations of powers of the world; knows what it means to hunger, to suffer physical pain, misunderstandings, the oppression of political conniving. He knows what it means to have to submit to laws which really do not fit. He knows the anguish of living in a milieu which he cannot change even though it is not as it should be. All these things he knew, for they are part of the human condition. It must be meaningful, therefore, even beautiful, to be human. I can see this from Jesus's life. If the Son of God chose to live our life, then our life must be meaningful.

Christ our Brother shared more with us than our humanity, however; he who is "the radiant light of God's glory and the perfect copy of his nature, sustaining the universe by his powerful command" (Heb 1:3) shared with us what was his own—the love of his Father and the *kabod* of Yahweh, the awesome majesty of God. He shared with us his gift of filiation: we are children of the Father, inspired by the Holy Spirit, and we are at home in the Blessed Trinity. Much more than merely human beings, we are children of God, brothers of Christ, temples of the Holy Spirit, witnesses to his truth and his love. And because of these gifts, we in our turn can bring life and warmth to the people.

In one sense, the incarnation took place at a given moment in time. But we can also say that the incarnation is an on-going process; there is always more to be achieved. At each moment of his incarnate existence we find Christ completely himself, fully God and fully man, but always there was more of the mystery of his incarnation to be unfolded. At Nazareth he took flesh in Mary's womb, but there he was a human fetus needing to develop before he would be a full-fledged man. At the moment of his birth in Bethlehem he was visibly and existentially present among us, but he was as yet only a baby, needing to grow to adulthood in order to take on the tasks of a man. It requires a lifetime for us to attain the full potential of our humanity, and this was true of Christ also. With each action, each experience, he became more completely the person he had willed to be: a man growing more rich and more fruitful in his humanity as he lived out the ordinary routine of his life. In one way we may say that at Calvary his life had come to fulfillment. Even Christ had said this of himself, and the gospels often reflect the same truth, considering his consummation on Calvary as *the hour* of his life, the hour in which he drew to himself all men and reached his peak—his death which leads into his resurrection. But then, even after his resurrection there is still much to grow. The incarnation has not yet reached its fulfillment in the resurrection of Christ. He is the vine, we the branches. Without the branches, the vine is not complete. Christ is the life within us, and he has to grow in each of us. Thus his Mystical Body grows and expands. In Teilhard de Chardin's vision, the whole of mankind is on the way to an ever greater unity with Christ, in whom evolution reaches point Omega and the incarnation achieves its pleroma. The human race will be accomplished in him, and he in the human race. The true meaning of man's life and the purpose of the world is that Christ may become more and more the All-in-all. Each of us has to grow into a true image of Christ and to become a living *sequentia sancti Evangelii,* as the old liturgy of the Mass expressed it, so that the world at large may be filled ever more with the presence of the risen Lord. That is the meaning and purpose of both the individual and the collective existence of mankind. Even the whole of creation itself is directed towards this goal: "From the beginning till now the entire creation, as we know, has been groaning in one great act of giving birth..." (Rom 8:22). St. Paul often develops thoughts along these lines:

God has put all things under Christ's feet, and made him, as the ruler of everything, the head of the Church; which is his body, the fullness of him who fills the whole creation (Eph 1:22-23).

All baptised in Christ, you have all clothed yourselves in Christ, and there are no more distinctions between Jew and Greek, slave and free, male and female, but all of you are one in Christ Jesus (Gal 3:26-28).

Now the Church is his body,
he is its head.
As he is the Beginning,
he was first to be born from the dead,
so that he should be first in every way;
because God wanted the *pleroma*
to be found in him (Col 1:18-19).

After that will come the end, when Christ hands over the kingdom to God the Father, having done away with every sovereignty, authority, and power. For he must be king until he has put all his enemies under his feet and the last of the enemies to be destroyed is death, for everything is to be put under his feet. ...And when everything is subjected to him, then the Son himself will be subject in his turn to the One who subjected all things to him, so that God may be all in all (1 Cor 15:24-28).

In a sense, there is only one happening in this world: the incarnation. The apotheosis of this will be the complete Christ, incorporating all humanity in himself and clothed with the universe as with a robe, abandoning himself to his Father.

From Mary we can learn total receptivity in order that this total incarnation may continue in and through us. We can pray for ourselves and for each other, that Christ incarnate may enliven and deepen the meaningfulness of our own life and of all creation. This prayer easily turns into a truly apostolic prayer also since the best wish we can ever have for another is that he discover more who Christ is and how he is the *one* Person we are all longing for, whether we know his name or not.

Nine

USE YOUR TALENTS

In our contemplation on the life of Jesus in order to fathom God's Word, we are impressed by the noteworthy fact that ninety percent of his life was passed in the obscure little town of Nazareth. St. Luke is explicit:

> When Mary and Joseph had done everything the Law of the Lord required, they went back to Galilee, to their own town of Nazareth. Meanwhile the child grew to maturity, and he was filled with wisdom; and God's favor was with him (Lk 2:39-40).

> He then went down with them and came to Nazareth and lived under their authority. His mother stored up all these things in her heart. And Jesus increased in wisdom, in stature, and in favor with God and men (Lk 2:51-52).

The hidden years at Nazareth constitute an opaque episode, a real mystery, and like all the mysteries in the life of Christ and in God's revelation, it is inscrutable; we can never sound its full depth. Yet in the gospels there are no riddles for riddles' sake. Hence, although I cannot wholly grasp it, there is still a message in Nazareth which I somehow have to decipher and to realize, for the penetration of this enigma, like all gospel mysteries, is more than a flight of fancy. It is an invitation to share more intimately in Christ's understanding of his mission and to continue this carefully in my own life.

CALLED BY NAME

The message and the mystery of Nazareth are not easy to absorb. In fact, there are those who have become angry at it, as though it were a summons to an unwarranted subservience or even worse, to a servile acquiescence with the status-quo of the establishment. This reaction may be preferable, however, to a too ready acceptance of the thirty years spent at Nazareth, one which does not take seriously enough that for all those years the warning of the Baptist holds true: "...there stands among you,—unknown to you,—the one who is coming after me" (Jn 1:26). If such a large segment of the life of Jesus was spent in the obscurity of Nazareth, then I must digest this fact, ponder it, try to understand its root meaning for me and for all Christians.

One of the most obvious notes about Nazareth is its obscurity. It was a backward little village, cut off from the centers of the world of those days. In Rome, where the political and military power resided, almost no one had ever heard of Nazareth; in sophisticated Athens, outstanding for its intellectual and cultural tradition, they did not know it at all. And the people of Nazareth in their turn had no idea of these large metropolitan centers. Each year the families of Nazareth would make their prescribed journey to Jerusalem, which for them seemed a large city although for the Romans Jerusalem was a place of scorn, a troublesome city of the Empire with odd people whom they could never figure out, and the men of Athens looked down on the whole of Palestine, dismissing its inhabitants as backward, unsophisticated people lacking all culture. Yet it was at Nazareth that Jesus chose to spend so many years among these people who never knew how limited they were. At no time did Jesus ever cross the borders of his own very small country; within the narrow, unpromising confines of Palestine he lived his entire life and carried out the mission entrusted to him by his Father: "to bear witness to the truth" (Jn 18:37).

The life Jesus passed in Nazareth seemed to correspond completely with its setting. Here he practised hidden virtues, lived under authority, was dependent. It was a simple life, in many ways slow and boring, lacking the sensational and the exciting. There was the daily round of work and prayer and simple joys or sorrows, the enervating sameness of place and persons and incidents, with little to vary the routine or to lift consciousness beyond the limits of the local region. It was as though the outside world did not exist. And what did Jesus do in this quiet village? He lived under authority! Perhaps this is one of the most difficult aspects of his life for us to accept in our times. A contemporary missalette prepared for use in European parish churches illustrates well the resistance which this quality in Christ's life arouses today. The Communion antiphon for the Feast of the Holy Family, which in the new liturgy is observed on the last Sunday of the year, contains the Latin phrase from the gospel: *Descendit Jesus cum eis et venit Nazareth et erat subditus illis.* For several years this particular missalette has translated this antiphon: "Jesus went with them to Nazareth, where he stayed with them in commitment and faithfulness." But that is not what either the Latin or the Greek text says. We may not like it, but what the gospel says is *erat subditus illis*—he lived under their authority.

What Christ was called upon to practise at Nazareth was the heroism of the ordinary, the daily routine which requires its own kind of courage. The prior of a Carthusian monastery has written some revealing comments on the true nature of the courage which a life of religious commitment can demand. The Carthusians are recognized as probably the most austere Order within the Church, and this particular monastery had a large number of candidates offering themselves generously for its rigorous life. The custom was to welcome the candidates and then let them decide whether they would go at once to their hermitage or would prefer to spend some time of transition in the guest house. The majority chose to withdraw immediately to the hermitages. This made sense, of course, for the very austerity of the life seemed to insure that only the most fervent young men would be coming to the Carthusians. The prior visited them daily, their sole contact with other persons. Quite often on the second or third day, some of the young candidates expressed disappointment: the life was too easy. In their dreams they had imagined a far more austere life, but the one they were living seemed too simple. The prior would say to himself: "This man will not persevere; he will leave, but for the opposite reason." The prior would continue his daily visits, and sure enough after two or three weeks he would arrive one day to find the candidate in extreme agitation: he would leave immediately; he could wait no longer. The life was impossible, utterly beyond endurance. It was so austere—everything was lacking. So he would leave—and for the opposite reasons, as the prior had foreseen.

We should not laugh at the dilemma of these young men, nor even smile, for what they are discovering is something essential for any religious life: *viz.*, it is at once too humble for our pride and too exacting for the sensual man. The young candidate who leaves precipitously has had to face this challenge and has found himself unequal to it. Before he entered, he had been the hero, going to join the Order that is so severe. As soon as he is in the monastery, however, there is no one to admire him; they are all Carthusians! Then he discovers that religious life is too small for our pride. The chair of a hero may not be a comfortable seat, but at least in it one has a sense of heroism. In the hermitage there is no such chair, the young man discovers, and he is left with a feeling of disenchantment. But there is still more to come, for after a few weeks he discovers that the life is, after all, a rather meager one—too exacting for our senses. It is not precisely an easy, contented life. This means that he is bereft both of the chair of the hero and of the chair of comfort. This is too much—and he leaves. It may be that Christ experienced something like this at Nazareth. Too small for our pride: there was nothing special about his daily life—no one to admire him, no one even to pay any special attention to him. And too meager for our senses: it was a frugal life, simple and with little human satisfaction. Yet Jesus persevered. He was experiencing for himself—and here we touch something of what the mystery has to communicate to us—that the narrowness and austerity of Nazareth were an indispensable part of the mission entrusted to him by his Father.

There is another aspect of Christ's hidden life which we must consider in some depth if we are to come to terms with the mystery of Nazareth. St. Luke tells us that here Christ "grew to maturity," a phrase that reveals layers of meaning and helps us to comprehend a little of the miracle of growth and human development taking place in Christ. Here at Nazareth among relatives and associates of his childhood and youth Christ attained through imitation and experience those qualities which characterized him throughout his life and made him recognizable for what he was—a man of Nazareth. He acquired the speech patterns and intonations, the mannerisms and physical stamina, the psychological reactions and social responses which formed the later prophet of Capernaum and Jerusalem. Moreover, all this was not merely an external alteration of a facade; it was a true *growth*, a day by day development that gradually transformed Christ, modifying and changing him with each new phase. Nor was the development limited only to observable phenomena, for the years of Nazareth were a time of unbelievable interior growth. John Haughey has developed at some length the meaning of these years in Nazareth which not only served to bring him to the age acceptable to proclaim the Kingdom or to teach him to communicate with people. Most of all they were years in which Jesus discovered who he was, that he was child, son, only son of his Father:

> Jesus' knowledge of God and his knowledge of himself grew apace. The more certain he became that God was loving, the more he knew that he was loved. As the personality of God became manifestly that of a loving Father, Jesus learned that he was a beloved son. With infinite skill, the Spirit taught him to differentiate between Himself and others, and understand that he was a son in a way no one else ever was or would be. He discovered who he was by discovering that God was his Father...Having understood himself and his own heart, he developed an ability which became evident in his public life, of piercing to the hearts of his hearers.[1]

So, as he grew at Nazareth Jesus became who he was. He needed those years not just to relate to people or to

speak a language comprehensible to them, but most of all
to know who he was himself and to grow in awareness of
God as his Father, discovering in all this the message he
was to communicate to us. It may seem remarkable that
Jesus needed thirty years for this, but we shall make that
judgment only if we underestimate the reality of growth in
his life.

There is still more depth, however, to the mystery of
Nazareth. Charles de Foucauld, whose spirituality is perhaps one of the most fruitful of this century, has chosen
Nazareth as the focal point of his own spiritual life and
doctrine. In itself, this seems somewhat remarkable, for if
we were to place the question: "In this twentieth century,
the age of space-craft and nuclear energy, of T-groups and
sociology, what is the most appealing passage of the
gospel?" few would ever expect that the answer would be
Nazareth. And yet we must agree that de Foucauld, whose
spirituality is based so firmly on the mystery of Nazareth,
has had singular impact on the religious dimension of our
age. He had gone there literally, had lived there, trying to
absorb the atmosphere and to re-create the experience of
Christ; and he had understood how truly Christ had taken
the lowest place. St. Luke tells us that Jesus "went down
to Nazareth." His whole life was a going down. He went
down by becoming man; went down by becoming a little
child; went down by being obedient; went down by
making himself poor and helpless, expelled and persecuted
and eventually executed; went down by always taking the
last place. He who was to teach: "When you are a guest,
make your way to the lowest place and sit there" (Lk
14:10), began by himself taking the lowest seat at the feast
of life, a place he held until his death. He came to

Nazareth, the scene of a hidden life, to the ordinary, everyday life of a family, made up of a round of prayer and work, insignificant, marked only by hidden virtues, and only God and his closest relatives and neighbors were witnesses to any of it. Nazareth is the place of a wholly beneficent but inglorious life, the life of the majority of people. There we learn that it is the lowest place that we are to seek if we are to find a place near Christ.

There is a further message from Nazareth, in many ways the most perplexing of all, for it seems to present a contradiction. We may be annoyed by the mystery and may even argue against it, using the gospel itself to refute its thesis. Doesn't the gospel teach that I must make the best use of my talents? "No one lights a lamp to put it under a tub; they put it on the lamp-stand where it shines for everyone in the house" (Mt 5:15). These words of Jesus explicitly caution that I must not hide my light, yet at Nazareth that is exactly what he himself did! He is not consistent, therefore, and I am going to contest his example. Thus I shall be free of the scandal of Nazareth, for on the message of the gospel itself I shall base my conviction that talents are to be used, not hidden. In support of my position I can cite also the Parable of the Talents, where the man producing most receives the greatest reward, and the man who hid his one talent is condemned (Mt 25:14-30).

It is true that we must make use of our talents; the apparent contradiction seems puzzling. But the question really is: What does "talents" mean? It is here that we often misunderstand. I may have a talent for teaching mathematics. I want to study that discipline—and then I expect a post where I can teach the subject. Or I may have

116

a talent for administration, and I am convinced that the Order should capitalize on this. Or I may have a talent for art or music or ballet. I should develop my talent to the full, become a real ballet dancer! But is this really what the gospel means? The heart of our talents is not that we can teach or play or dance; important as these accomplishments are, they are only secondary. We do not know what talents of this kind Jesus had, but if he had any, he did waste them. There is another talent, however, the one Jesus really had, and this is the deep meaning of Nazareth:

> Make your home in me, as I make mine in you.
> As a branch cannot bear fruit all by itself,
> but must remain part of the vine,
> neither can you unless you remain in me (Jn 15:4).

This is the real talent—to remain in God. It alone is the core, and anything else is subordinate. If we lose the basic talent, then all others are worthless. Jesus used his talent well: he lived in his Father, rooted so firmly in him that even during his public life it was his Father who meant everything to him. Indeed, "remain in my love!" Unless I remain in God, I waste all my talents, and having squandered them, I shall truly have a hard time at the Judgment.

The "real talent" then is on the fundamental level, and it remains invisible to the eyes of men; only ". . .your Father who sees all that is done in secret will reward you" (Mt 6:4,6). This is what Jesus lived and made most of in Nazareth. And it is in this that we have to follow him: ". . .you have died, and now the life you have is hidden with Christ in God. But when Christ is revealed—and he is your life—you too will be revealed in all your glory with him" (Col 3:3-4). If we are sincerely open to it, the mystery of Nazareth tells us what really counts: "Not that it makes the slightest difference to me whether you, or indeed any human tribunal, find me worthy or not. I will not even pass judgment on myself. True, my conscience does not reproach me at all, but that does not prove that I am acquitted: the Lord alone is my judge" (1 Cor 4:3-4). It was this hidden use of talents that Thomas Merton prayed for when he asked:

> Untie my hands and deliver my heart from sloth. Set me free from the laziness that goes about disguised as activity when activity is not required of me, and from the cowardice that does what is not demanded, in order to escape a sacrifice. But give me the strength that waits upon you in silence and peace. Give me humility in which alone is rest, and deliver me from pride which is the heaviest of burdens. And possess my whole heart and soul with the simplicity of love. Occupy my whole life with the one thought and the one desire of love. . . .[2]

What then is the real talent? "Then the Jews said to Jesus: 'What must we do if we are to do the works that God wants?' Jesus gave them this answer: 'This is working for God: you must believe in the one he has sent' " (Jn 6:28-29). This is what working for God means, the basic talent: to believe in Christ. It is that which has priority and must be developed; all others are secondary and must yield place. The lesson of Nazareth, therefore, becomes crystal clear: God really takes precedence in everything. I may need time and hiddenness for this; I may need to be in the lowest place for quite a while in order to let the conviction grow within me that God is really the all-important in my life. It is for this that I have to go to my Nazareth.

Use Your Talents

During the years in Nazareth apparently only one thing happened that is worthy of mention: his stay in the temple when his parents did not know of it. And the core of this mystery is exactly the same as the whole life in Nazareth. The essence of the mystery of what happened in the temple brings home to Mary and Joseph—and to each of us—that the personality of Jesus cannot be understood from the milieu in which he was born and reared, but only from his relation with God whom he calls "Father." Once again we find that the heart of his life and his mission was his Father. He comes from the Father and lives for him alone. It is this which gives infinite depth, real fruitfulness to his life, and because his roots penetrate so deeply into his Father, he can reach out so far to the people. This is the whole essence of his life. In Christ there was no shred of self-concern because he knew that his Father took care of him. He was absolutely sure of the favor of his Father. This was the atmosphere in which he lived, the air he breathed; therefore, he needed no self-concern, in fact he could have none. As a result, his full attention and love could go out to others. Had Jesus not retreated this far into loneliness with his Father, he would never have been able to associate with people as freely as he did. In the temple, therefore, we find once again the whole core of the mystery of Nazareth in his answer: "Why were you looking for me? . . .Did you not know that I must be busy with my Father's affairs?" In a flash of illumination Mary understood that the ruling preoccupation in the life of Jesus was with God whom he called his Father.

We can say of Mary that the moment in which she had found her Son was really the moment in which she lost him forever. It was then that she realized that Jesus was far more the Son of the Father than her son. Mary loses her son because it turns out that the child has another Father who lives in heaven, and with the realization of this a new dimension comes into her faith:

> The significance of Mary's virginity may pale in importance by comparison to her ability to accept the complete otherness of her son without erasing any of his uniqueness which she could not fully understand. Scripture takes note of Mary's capacity for pondering events and others' words. . .She receives them in their otherness.[3]

Mary received Jesus as he is—and that means different, not different as any one human being is from another, but completely different: the Son of God in the full sense of the word. Jesus of Nazareth is led by the Will of his Father; that is the food on which he lives. In a certain sense, we can say that when Jesus leaves the temple of Jerusalem, he takes the temple with him. The house of his Father is where he lives at all times, even in Nazareth. Always he shows an awareness of his intimate communion with God which makes his whole life like a temple. That is why he can say later at the cleansing of the temple in Jerusalem: "Destroy this temple and in three days I will raise it up" (Jn 2:19 NAB). He was speaking of his own body at this time, and his words were accurate. Because he lived always in his Father, he was truly the living temple. This is the mystery of the first thirty years of his life, both of the hiddenness and of that one event which Luke thought worth recording.

Ten

PUT TO THE TEST

The early Church was strongly convinced that Christ had really been tempted and that in his temptations we can gain clear insight into the personality of Jesus. The very placement of the account of the temptations immediately after the narrative of the baptism, which originally formed the opening of the synoptic gospels, indicates the importance which the evangelists saw in the incident. They were convinced that the reality of temptation in Christ's life implies a comforting message for Christians since both the fact of his temptation and the sublime manner in which he reacted against it constitute for us a source of encouragement and strength, the Good News of Christ: "For it is not as if we had a high priest who was incapable of feeling our weaknesses with us; but we have one who has been tempted in every way that we are, though he is without sin" (Heb 4:15). There we have the two elements of the Good News concerning Jesus:

a) he has been tempted in every way that we are:

It was essential that he should in this way become completely like his brothers so that he could be a compassionate and trustworthy high priest of God's religion, able to atone for human sins. That is, because he has himself been through temptation he is able to help others who are tempted (Heb 2:17-18).

b) in all this he still remained without sin. One of our race has managed not to yield in the least to the seductions of evil. This is a source of joy for us.

We must be realists in our considerations of this mystery of Christ's temptation to evil, however, or we shall deny the truth of his nature—one like to us in everything save sin. The temptations in the life of Christ were genuine; the seduction to misuse his power was ever present, constituting for him an actual danger. Throughout his entire life, even to its very end, Jesus had to face decisions as to the meaning and the spirit of his own mission. In all these decisions, however, he remained faithful to the Will of his Father. When we speak of the temptations of Christ inevitably we think immediately of the elaborate account given by Matthew and Luke of the temptations in the desert. There are many other instances, however, scattered throughout the whole life of Christ. If that were not the case, the letter to the Hebrews could scarcely say that he had been tempted in every way that we are. An incident in the desert, no doubt, seems a special kind of temptation, but the ordinary ones of daily life can be much more difficult to cope with. These too are found in the gospel. We shall consider six special incidents among many others.[1]

It is Matthew who describes the first incident, one of the high points of the public life of Christ (Mt 16:13-23).

When Jesus came to the region of Caesarea Philippi he put this question to his disciples, 'Who do people say the Son of Man is?' And they said, 'Some say he is John the Baptist, some Elijah, and others Jeremiah or one of the prophets.' 'But you,' he said, 'who do you say I am?' Then Simon Peter spoke up, 'You are the Christ,' he said, 'the Son of the living God.'

The answer was momentous because it revealed that after having been some time with Jesus the disciples have discovered who he really is, and Peter is able to verbalize this for them all. Jesus responds enthusiastically to Peter's words:

> Simon son of Jonah, you are a happy man! Because it was not flesh and blood that revealed this to you but my Father in heaven. So I now say to you: You are Peter and on this rock I will build my Church.

Once the apostles seem to have understood who Christ is, they are ready for further revelation, and from this moment onward Christ begins to speak of his passion. Having discovered who he is, they must now be prepared for the scandal of his cross. After this profession of Peter, therefore, comes the first explicit prophecy of the passion:

> From that time Jesus began to make it clear to his disciples that he was destined to go to Jerusalem and suffer grievously at the hands of the elders and chief priests and scribes, to be put to death and to be raised up on the third day. Then taking him aside, Peter started to remonstrate with him. 'Heaven preserve you, Lord,' he said, 'this must not happen to you.'

Peter's words really implied an attempt to keep Christ away from his passion, so Jesus "turned and said to Peter, 'Get behind me, Satan! You are an obstacle in my path, because the way you think is not God's way but man's.'" The reaction of Christ is vehement because he recognizes the incident for what it truly is—a temptation to prefer human success to human suffering. Christ words his rejection exactly: "the way you think is not God's but man's." Peter's temptation is very reasonable, very human.

This constitutes its greatest danger. Every temptation is reasonable. If it were not, it would not really be tempting. There is always something good, something sensible about evil to which we are enticed. That is its very allurement, what makes it attractive. It is man's way of thinking, not God's. The lines are sharply drawn here: Peter is judging by human standards, but Christ is led by the Will of the Father. Christ's reaction is so vehement because Peter here has touched the very nerve of his life: his Father's Will. Peter has attempted to substitute a human way of thinking for this divine Will, which is the only food Christ lives on and which means everything to him.

It is one of the dangers of our human situation that our way of thinking can and frequently does create illusions. The history of the Church illustrates well this foible: even the greatest minds have had their illusions. In the previous passage Christ has called God the author of Peter's discovery. Now we see that even a mind so enlightened can lose its grasp on truth. It is as though in the first response Peter was acknowledging Jesus as the Christ, the Son of God, implying that he wanted to follow him. But in the second passage he suggests that now he has become the leader, knowing what is best, and Jesus is really to become his follower. Peter has it all figured out. The incident represented a genuine temptation against which Christ had to react vehemently, and he did so by a sharp rejection of an all too human proposal.

There is even greater subtlety about the second temptation. "The Pharisees and Sadducees came, and to test him they asked if Jesus would show them a sign from heaven" (Mt 16:1). A sign from heaven—this surely was a reasonable enough request. He was coming, purporting to be the messiah, and all they asked was that he give proof of his authenticity. The scribes and Pharisees, well versed in scripture, had built up for themselves from their studies a picture of the messiah to come. All they sought now was that Christ give some indication that he really corresponded to this description. The danger of the request went deep, however, touching the very nature of Christ's being, for the picture that had been derived was not wholly reliable; scripture had been twisted a little, had yielded some illusions, and it was this distortion which constituted the great snare for Christ. There was the impulse to answer their expectations. This is always a temptation: to live up to the anticipations of others, to yield to human respect and fulfill their notions rather than to be truly ourselves. We must not think that Christ was insensible to the seduction of human success, the attraction to be 'with it.' And yet, what leads him, what governs his life is always the same: the Will of the Father. That is why he reacts against this temptation of the scribes and Pharisees: Why do you try to trap me? Why do you seduce me? It is the Will of the Father, not the expectations of men, which controls the life of Christ. On this Will he is to build the kingdom of God.

It was in the shadows of Gethsemane that one of the most powerful of his temptations was encountered by Christ.

> And going on a little further he threw himself on the ground and prayed that, if it were possible, this hour might pass him by. 'Abba (Father)!' he said, 'Everything is possible for you. Take this cup away from me. But let it be as you, not I would have it' (Mk 14:35-36).

Here the temptation is a genuine struggle, an agony. If we weigh these words on a gold scale, one that registers almost imperceptible variations, we find that Christ prays first to be spared this cup before he surrenders to his Father. Weighed on the same gold scale, we see Christ, who had always prized his unity with the Father—"I and the Father are one"—setting up a little opposition: "Let it be as you, not I, would have it." Even in this opposition, however, there is still surrender: "let it be as you. . .would have it." This moment in the life of Christ during which he contemplated so close at hand the agony and the horror of his death constituted one of his most searing trials. He had to fight even to the point of sweating blood in order to remain faithful to his mission. The Lord was not speaking idly when he said, "You should be awake and praying not to be put to the test. The spirit is willing, but the flesh is weak" (Mk 14:39). It was because he had been thus tested that he knew the force of this kind of trial, and he would have us see in his experience that such temptations can be rejected only in an agony.

Not all the temptations are encountered by Christ when he is in full control of the situation. Even during his last moments, when he was dying on the cross in fearful agony, he was not free from these assaults of evil. There he had to endure the torments of the passers-by who jeered at him: "they shook their heads and said, 'So you would destroy the temple and rebuild it in three days! Then save yourself! If you are God's Son, come down from the cross!' " (Mt 27:40). These are the very words Satan had used in the desert: If you are God's Son, let the stones become loaves of bread, throw yourself down from the parapet of the Temple! There is no change now in that relentless pursuit: If you are God's Son, come down from the cross. It is the fundamental challenge in which his own identity is questioned. If you are the Son of God, then do this or that. The temptation must have been strong to come down from the cross and to crush his enemies, proving by his rescue that he really is the Son of God. But Christ proves this not by coming down, but by staying on the cross. In this way he convinces some, like the Roman centurion: "In truth this man was a son of God" (Mk 15:39). And on the cross, as in the more ordinary events of his life, Christ shows that the one thing that truly matters is fidelity to our God-given self, even in the midst of temptations.

From the variety of the temptations encountered by Christ we can understand how truly the letter to the Hebrews spoke: "He was tempted in every way." In the pressures to manifest outwardly his prowess Jesus encountered even in his own family a source of temptation.

> As the Jewish feast of Tabernacles drew near, his brothers said to him, 'Why not leave this place and go to Judaea, and let your disciples see the works you are doing; if a man wants to be known he does not do things in secret; since you are doing all this, you should let the whole world see' (Jn 7:2-9).

The situation is intensely, even appealingly, human. Christ is working miracles, and his relatives are experiencing a certain fascination; it is truly exciting to have a cousin who can perform such marvels. Certainly, this could be a help in their own careers! But the trouble is that this strange cousin insists upon working his miracles in Galilee, a backward province. Why not in Jerusalem, where his prowess would really count? A man who wants to be known does not operate in secret! And so the family begins its assault, putting pressure on Jesus to come out into the open, to manifest himself more publicly. John adds the significant comment: "Not even his brothers, in fact, had faith in him." Their concern for him to become known, therefore, was no indication that they believed in him; rather, it was a desire for personal profit. They might easily draw some advantages from his skills. Once again, however, Jesus repulsed the merely natural approach, the seduction of human politics. It was the Spirit of God which should dominate him, and so without rancor he replied:

> The right time for me has not come yet, but any time is the right time for you. . . .Go up to the festival yourselves: I am not going to this festival, because for me the time is not ripe yet.

John adds: "Having said that, he stayed behind in Galilee."

The temptations we have considered thus far have been, in a sense, attempts to seduce the mind of Christ. The final one, however, takes the form of a threat of bodily harm, the last refuge of the cowardly oppressor:

> Just at this time some Pharisees came up. 'Go away,' they said. 'Leave this place, because Herod means to kill you.' He replied, 'You may go and give that fox this message: Learn that today and tomorrow I cast out devils and on the third day attain my end. But for today and tomorrow and the next day I must go on, since it would not be right for a prophet to die outside Jerusalem' (Lk 13:31-33).

The threat, actually attributed to Herod, is reported to Jesus by the Pharisees, but it in no way deflects him from his purpose. He will yield neither to political pressure nor to threats to his own person. "Learn that today and tomorrow I cast out devils, and on the third day I attain my end." The "third day" means very soon, and Jesus knows this, but he knows too that on this day he will "attain his end"—a word full of meaning since it includes both his death and the achievement of his mission. Jesus was made perfect by his suffering and death, and he knows this will come soon so he remains faithful. "I must go on." Not even fear of death can turn him aside. Like the others, this temptation will fail.

These six examples should suffice to show how Christ was tempted in his daily life just as we are. What was at stake was always the method of the apostolate. It was never the kingdom of God itself which was questioned but only the way in which Christ was to bring this kingdom about. The temptation was to take the crown without the cross, to establish the kingdom by way of human success rather than by way of failure, to elect popularity rather than suffering and even death, to choose the shallow, selfish approach rather than to follow God's Will for him: these were the temptations for Christ. They were real, and he had to struggle against them. We misunderstand completely if we think the victory was easy.

The confrontation of Christ and Satan, described at length by Matthew and Luke and referred to by Mark, forms a kind of summary of the major temptations in the life of Jesus which persisted throughout his life, but were concentrated in the evangelists' accounts in order to underscore their seductiveness and their danger. The setting is impressive: Jesus and Satan in the desert—and nothing else. It is an encounter between the two powers which rule in this world; anything secondary is taken away. Here there is laid bare the essence of all temptation, for in the lives of each of us these same two powers clash. Mark says that it was the Spirit which drove Christ into the desert (Mk 1:12). The temptations, therefore, were not a mistake; they are a necessary part of discipleship, belonging to the life of Christ and to ours. The struggle occurs in the desert, a place in which there is no escape. In its vastness there is loneliness, no one to understand or to sympathize, no one even to disagree. It is a place where I can achieve nothing. Perhaps this is the most difficult trial of all: not to be able to accomplish anything. Even if I were able to achieve some little thing, were it only to build castles in the sand, there would be no one to admire my work. There is only loneliness. The desert is literally the place of truth, bringing me face to face with the real inspiration of my life. The Little Brothers and Sisters of Jesus actually go into the desert, not for just a brief excursion, but for a long sojourn. It is rather exciting to make this trip for a few days; when the stay is prolonged, however, the excitement is soon over and the test begins. René Voillaume writes with understanding of this experience:

> In the loneliness we can make a periodic clearance of the illusions which prevent us from obtaining a clear view of all the things that clutter up our heart. One cannot be in the desert for any serious length of time if one is not simple and poor in spirit and if one expects from life something other than God alone. That is why the temptation to make ourselves useful to men in another way than just to show God's greatness and love, the temptation to establish the kingdom of God by any other means than the ones Jesus used, can ultimately be overcome only in the desert as Jesus did.[2]

If I seek God and God only, then I can go into the desert unafraid because I can be sure that God is there. If, however, I expect more from life than God alone, then I must not go to the desert, for that more which I am seeking cannot be found there. The desert is the testing ground for authenticity. There I can know for certain what it is that I am seeking—God alone or God plus something else. Do I serve one master, or are there really two? In the desert there is only one Master, and the apparent sterility of my work there may be the only way to insure that it is truly this Master whom I serve.

> To seek too much human fulfillment while the gift of virginity is taking root may cut short a developing special friendship with God. The friends of God have always been trained and tested in some sort of desert; it may have been symbolic, it may have been spiritual, but desert it was. It can be bypassed only in the imagination of some, never in reality. Not even Christ bypassed it.[3]

The three temptations of Christ in the desert yield a clear insight into the personality of Jesus: he served the Father in true self-renunciation. The temptations were hardly subtle. "If you are the son of God, tell these stones to turn into loaves." How strong is this appeal to the basic desire of man—the desire to grasp rather than to receive, to have our own life under control rather than to live open-handedly. To look upon God's providence as a means of putting God at the ready service of our daily needs would be a specious form of abandonment to his care, a recourse to a kind of magic. Miracles can never be the basis of our confidence in God; we must simply trust, no matter what the circumstances. In an affluent society there is ever present the urge to take in whatever you can—that is temptation. To live with open hands, letting God take out and put in as he wills—that is living in God's providence. The favor of the Father was not to make life easier for Christ; he too had to await the hour of God, had to live in an attitude of receptivity rather than of grasping. This first of the desert temptations lets us see how he reacted so that we may better understand his way.

The second temptation is also direct, rather gross: "If you are the Son of God, throw yourself down,"—a temptation to bring the kingdom of God by human means: ostentation, meetings, setting up my own image to impress the people, an instant enthusiasm instead of a patient growth. We can easily confuse the burgeoning of our own popularity with the growth of the kingdom of God, yet the two are not identical. In fact, it may be that the kingdom of God advances in proportion to my decline in popularity. To seek to impress people, to solicit their approval, can be a very real temptation. Here in this second experience we see Christ showing us that the kingdom of God is built in humility, in looking for the last place, not the first.

In one sense, the last of the three temptations in the desert is the most vicious of all: "I will give you all these if you fall at my feet and worship me"—that is, the temptation to worship something other than God. The very last words of John in his letter to the early Church are a warning against this same hazard: "Children, be on your guard against idols" (1 Jn 5:21). Pride is rarely open rebellion against God; that would be stupid. It is always placing something next to God, an attempt to set up two masters, to identify something less than the divine with God—not theoretically, of course, but in practice—an effort to synthesize something foreign with God or with his kingdom. Once we have in fact put an idea or principle on the divine level, in the name of this false value we shall find ourselves subjecting everything else to it, and this means, indeed, that we have erected it into an idol to which we are prepared to sacrifice all. Until this moment in his ordeal in the desert Jesus has remained calm, low-keyed, but at the suggestion of idolatry he becomes inflamed, furious: "Get off, Satan. . . !" It is God alone who is to be adored.

In each instance in the desert Jesus overcomes the temptation by turning to his Father: man does not live by bread alone, but by every word that comes from the mouth of God; man should not put God to the test; man must adore God and serve him alone. In an act of adoration man is able to break through the "reasonableness" that makes temptation seductive:

> Jesus knew that once He removed his eye from the glory and praise of the Father, many things could be justified as serving the mission for which he was sent. The kingdom that he preached would then become something of this world, and the execution of his mission a way of serving himself. If the Son did not seek to glorify the Father, he would seek to glorify himself. . . .the Spirit teaches Jesus what he had to learn: the difference between being a sign and being a spectacle; between pointing to himself and witnessing to the Father; between redeeming the human by raising it up and escaping from the human by flight into spiritualism; between powers used for their own sake and those used for the sake of the Kingdom.[4]

The fact that Christ has conquered the world (Jn 16:33) assures us of the possibility we have of overcoming temptations in his strength. "You can trust God not to let you be tried beyond your strength, and with any trial he

133

will give you a way out of it and the strength to bear it" (1 Cor 10:13). In fact, as John assures us, the victory is already won:

> anyone who has been begotten by God
> has already overcome the world;
> this is the victory over the world—
> our faith (1 Jn 5:4).

Eleven

BUT I SAY THIS

During the struggle for independence in India it happened one day that Gandhi arrived at a railway station in the South where thousands of people were awaiting him. After descending from the train, he stood for quite a while, silent, unmoving. Finally, when urged to say something, he took from the folds of his garments a little booklet which turned out to be the New Testament, and from the gospel of Matthew he read aloud the eight Beatitudes. When he had finished, Gandhi waved his hand and said simply: "That is all I have to say; go home and ponder it."

In the Beatitudes we can find a compendium of the whole doctrine of Jesus. They form the core of the Sermon on the Mount, that compilation of teachings which the evangelist offers, a kind of inaugural address at the outset of Christ's ministry. Interestingly enough, the Sermon on the Mount is addressed in the first place to the apostles: "Seeing the crowds, Jesus went up the hill. There he sat down and was joined by his disciples. Then he began to speak. This is what he taught them: 'How happy are the poor in spirit. . .' " (Mt 5:1-3). In his parallel account Luke makes it even more obvious that the words are directed to the apostles:

Now it was about this time that he went out into the hills to pray; and he spent the whole night in prayer to God. When day came he summoned his disciples and picked out twelve of them; he called them 'apostles'. . . .He then came down with them and stopped at a piece of level ground. . .Then, fixing his eyes on his disciples he said, 'How happy are you who are poor. . .' (Lk 6:12-13, 17, 20).

Clearly, the Sermon is meant for the apostles. But both Matthew and Luke stress that there is a large crowd around the apostles, men and women who likewise share in this teaching. "Seeing the crowds, he went up the hill" (Mt).

He then came down with the apostles and stopped at a piece of level ground where there was a large gathering of his disciples with a great crowd of people from all parts of Judaea and from Jerusalem and from the coastal region of Tyre and Sidon who had come to hear him and to be cured of their diseases (Lk).

It is evident, therefore, that from his apostles Christ's doctrine flows to everybody. Jesus does not have a special doctrine reserved only for his friends, nor are there any demands made only of an elite; he offers an invitation and a challenge to everyone.

The Beatitudes are based on the example and words of Jesus himself, as if he were presenting in eight sure strokes a careful self-portrait. They are a summons to share the mind of Christ, an invitation to a life which I myself can never initiate, and Jesus is assuring me that the experience offers bliss, that it will fill me with happiness. Like the whole gospel, it is a gift offered freely, but it becomes real only when it is received and accepted. It is a gift of God, one such as the world can never give, but if I want to achieve this happiness, I must make myself receptive; I must listen with a ready heart to this word of God: "...none of you can be my disciple unless he gives up all his possessions" (Lk 14:33).

The Old Testament was a religion of listening. *The* great commandment which every Jew recited each morning and evening as his prescribed daily prayer began with the cry, *"Sjema Israel*: Listen, Israel: Yahweh our God is the one Yahweh..." (Deut 6:4). The Greek religions were based on *idein* (to see) which leads to ideas, views, insights. The Hebrew religion, on the contrary, was based on listening—a listening, that is, to the Word of God. There is a vast difference between human words and the divine Word. When *we* speak, there is always a certain distance between the word and the speaker. This can be painful enough because it implies that we can never express ourselves adequately in words. That is why we need so many words, trying always to come as close as possible to what we really mean to say. We can abuse that distance between the word and our true selves, hiding behind a host of words so as to form a kind of curtain to cover the essential. We can go further still in abusing the gap between the word and the heart by lying, using the words for the exact opposite of what we know to be true. The divine Word, however, is different. With God there is no division between himself and the Word he utters, for this Word is God himself in communication. In his Word God is completely present as the communicating God. Consequently, the Word of God differs in no way from God himself, nor is it less than God: "In the beginning was the Word: and the Word was with God and the Word was God. He was with God in the beginning" (Jn 1:1-2).

The Jew was admonished to listen to the Word of God with great reverence as if he were hearing it for the first time in his life, as if he were actually present on Mount Sinai, receiving the revelation directly from the mouth of God. On the Word of God depended the happiness of man. The psalms make this abundantly clear:

> I am listening. What is Yahweh saying?
> What God is saying means peace
> for his people, for his friends (Ps 85:8).

Listen, therefore, and you will be filled with that deep peace which the world cannot give, nor can the world take it away.

> The Law of Yahweh is perfect,
>   new life for the soul;
> the decree of Yahweh is trustworthy,
>   wisdom for the simple.

> The precepts of Yahweh are upright,
>   joy for the heart;
> the commandment of Yahweh is clear,
>   light for the eyes.

> More desirable than gold,
>   even than the finest gold;
> his words are sweeter than honey,
>   even than honey that drips from the comb (Ps 19:7-8,
>   10).

> Now your word is a lamp to my feet,
>   a light on my path (Ps 119:105).

Let me open myself to this word of God which means peace and happiness for my heart, for my whole being, and

I shall radiate true joy. If I do open my heart to this word, then something will surely happen to me, for "the word of God is something alive and active" (Heb 4:12).

> Yes, as the rain and the snow come down from the heavens and do not return without watering the earth, making it yield and giving growth to provide seed for the sower and bread for the eating, so the word that goes from my mouth does not return to me empty, without carrying out my will and succeeding in what it was sent to do (Is 55:10-11).

Because the word of God will achieve something in me, I can never listen to it in a detached, uncommitted way. To be receptive means to be willing to act accordingly. We could ask Mary to help us, Mary who was so receptive to the Word of God that it evoked in her the perfect response: she simply put her whole life at stake. Through her the Word of God came to earth and was made flesh: "At various times in the past and in various different ways, God spoke to our ancestors through the prophets: but in our own time, the last days, he has spoken to us through his Son...(Heb 1:1-2a). Now the Word of God could move in person over the earth: "...I saw Heaven open and a white horse appear; its rider was called Faithful and True....He is known by the name, the Word of God" (Rev 19:11-13).

In the Sermon on the Mount Matthew expresses in three separate ways that the Word was made flesh in Jesus. First, he draws a parallel between the Mount of the Beatitudes and Mount Sinai. The Old Testament was ratified on Mount Sinai; the New is proclaimed on the Mount of the Beatitudes. On Mount Sinai Yahweh was speaking to his people; in the Beatitudes it is again Yahweh who is speaking, this time through the Word incarnate.

Secondly, Matthew equates the authority with which Jesus speaks with the authority of Yahweh himself. Matthew was writing primarily for the Christians of Jewish descent who were accustomed not to pronounce the sacred name YHWH. At times they would substitute the term *Adonai* for YHWH. At other times they would use a passive circumlocution: "it was said to our ancestors. . ." meaning, "Yahweh said to our ancestors. . ." In the Sermon on the Mount we find several cases of parallel opposition: "You have learned how it was said to our ancestors. . ." (and all his readers understood, "You have learned how Yahweh said to our ancestors"), and "but I say this to you. . . ." The implication is obvious: Jesus has the same authority as Yahweh himself. Jesus has the right to speak like Yahweh, for he is the Word of God.

Lastly, Matthew stresses his point most explicitly in the final verse of the Sermon on the Mount: "Jesus had now finished what he wanted to say, and his teachings made a deep impression on the people because he taught them with authority, and not like their own scribes" (Mt 7:28-29). The Jews were accustomed to the instructional patterns of the scribes, who explained the meaning of scripture, supporting their interpretation with an appeal to tradition. Jesus speaks with an independent, divine authority, referring directly to Yahweh whom he calls his Father.

The tone of the Beatitudes is unambiguous: they are statements which announce something, but they make no demands. To be sure, these statements are revolutionary, for they inaugurate the foreshadowing of the heavenly Jerusalem: "Now I am making the whole of creation new" (Rev 21:5). Indeed, it is a wholly new outlook which Jesus introduces with these statements. It is an unfolding, an unveiling, which we could never have dreamed by ourselves. We need not be afraid that they are really a projection of ourselves, for had we created them, we can be sure they would have been quite different! Jesus speaks of bliss, but it is a kind of bliss that can be neither proved nor explained merely with the intellect. On the contrary, it can be fully grasped only to the degree that we embrace these Beatitudes as a way of life since it is only by living them that we shall discover how true they are. There is no other way.

Some people are called happy, and they are congratulated: "Good for you who are poor in spirit, who mourn, who hunger and thirst for what is right...." It is a happiness which is not *in* them, but one which comes *to* those who live this way. This happiness *is given*; it cannot be produced. Here again we find the passive construction: "They shall be comforted," meaning "God will comfort them"; "they shall be satisfied"; i.e., "God will satisfy them"; "they will have mercy shown to them"; i.e., "God will show them mercy." This happiness comes *to* us as a gift, not *from* us; and yet there is a profound relation between the happiness given and our innermost self. It is like a discovery, a coming home, a becoming more and more ourselves.

The whole tone of the Beatitudes is one of encouragement, so that they are a splendid antidote against despondency. Today there seems to be a great deal of dejection cropping up in all walks of life, including the religious life, fluctuating in range from the minimal to the maximal, and while the extent of the harm inflicted may vary between these extremes, the debilitating effects of this ennui can be serious. At one end of the scale we find the most seriously affected, those who have become sour, embittered, prostrated with trauma, filled with grudges

141

and resentment. Because so much in life has become for them a source of frustration, they seem unable to be constructive either for themselves or for others, and their outlook seems wholly negative. Any encouragement to a change of attitude is usually shrugged off pessimistically—*à quoi bon*?—and they seem unable or unwilling to make the effort. One of the tragic effects of this hopelessness is that no apostolate is possible in this situation, for such a life radiates not the good news but a stultifying, overwhelming sense of uselessness. At the other end of the scale this sense of despondency manifests itself in a kind of spiritual sloth—a life of compromise, of mediocrity: "I have this complaint to make; you have less love now than you used to" (Rev 2:4). Those pursuing this path are seeking a happy life and think to achieve it by conforming as much as possible to everybody else, doing what everyone else does, having as far as possible all that can be attained. The sad thing here is that religious of this type have really lost faith in their way of life. They do not leave, but they have missed what they came for. This too is a kind of despondency. They may try to convince others—and themselves—that they are really living and up-to-date, but deep down they are experiencing a life of disappointment and a lack of fulfillment.

These are only two of the possible forms which despondency may take. I do not want to judge, but merely to indicate that these instances of low spirits do occur, and for this I feel sorry. This is not the spirit of the vows; religious life is not meant to be like this. And because the Beatitudes are harbingers of joy, antidotes to the oppressive and the gloomy, Christ's Sermon on the Mount brings hope to such as these. Actually, the spirit of the Beatitudes can permeate man's whole being, transforming attitudes and effecting cures. Resentment can be cured, for example, because the Beatitudes really turn things upside down. What had been the cause of resentment is now seen as a source of blessedness. This is a revolutionary tactic. What do I resent? That I did not experience enough affection in my youth? I could spend a whole life brooding over this. But what does the Beatitude say? You are happy if this has happened to you because you can find God in a very special way. Or it may be that my resentment flows from a conviction that I have never been able to use all my talents to capacity. I can resent this, of course, but there is another possible reaction: I can rejoice. Happy are you! Or I may think that I have never really been understood, or that I was born at the wrong time—too early or too late. Happy are you! We have only to examine closely what it is that we resent, comparing this with the Beatitudes, and we shall find that what needs to be changed in our lives is not the circumstances but our attitude.

At the other end of the scale the Beatitudes can eradicate a certain callousness in our spiritual life; they can set afire again those who have lost their fervor. They can restore to dull, unhappy people the light that has been extinguished, and restore to the bland and the insipid the savor that has been lost.

> Our one desire is that everyone of you should go on showing the same earnestness to the end, to the perfect fulfillment of our hopes, never growing careless, but imitating those who have the faith and the perseverance to inherit the promises (Heb 6:11-12).

It is possible that the Beatitudes prove so encouraging and so inspiring just because they make no demands. They merely state that certain people are happy. They are not a law, but a gospel, Good News. They have no intention of laying a new yoke upon the disciples; rather they are offered as a simple but striking delineation of lived faith. It is as though the Beatitudes have a kind of presupposition, a preparation that comes before them and forms the core of the Good News; *viz.*, that we are loved by God and that our sins are forgiven; the kingdom of God has arrived; the time of salvation has come; the gifts of God surround us on all sides; behold, we are children of God and we may call him Father—and then on this basis rest the Beatitudes.

> Come to me, all you who labor and are overburdened, and I will give you rest. Shoulder my yoke and learn from me, for I am gentle and humble in heart, and you will find rest for your souls. Yes, my yoke is easy and my burden light (Mt 11:28-30).

One final general note about the Beatitudes: they are an example of a wholly positive outlook. They do not tear down, but rather build up. The real victory of evil consists often in the fact that it allures us into the very malice we are trying to resist, so that we become guilty of that wrong against which we are struggling. How often do we not oppose injustice by being unjust ourselves? How many who censure the Church for authoritarianism are themselves quite authoritarian both in their own behavior and in their attack? How easily do we write off people we are reproaching for having dismissed others too cavalierly? How many of the freedoms we claim are in fact addictions? How often do we not try to correct a bias by imposing an opposite bias? Evil can all too easily vanquish the champion for the good by putting into his hand the wrong weapon. It is one of the towering strengths of the Beatitudes that they preserve the good untarnished in the midst of evil, that they bring out the positive without any admixture of the negative. It is this which makes them revolutionary, not in the ordinary sense of the word—putting pressure on people or situations which only provokes counter-pressure, but rather by breaking through the vicious circle. It is not the doctrine of this world which the Beatitudes proclaim. Jesus rightly says: "Happy is the man who does not lose faith in me" (Mt 11:6). This is a different gospel from that we hear on all sides. It is a summons to a new way, and it takes much faith to carry on along this strange road.

Twelve

HAPPY ARE YOU

How happy are the poor in spirit; theirs is the kingdom of heaven. Interestingly enough, while all the other Beatitudes are in the future tense, this one is in the present. The poor have their treasure in heaven, where their Father is, and therefore, even now their heart and their home are in heaven as well. They experience a deep, all-pervading joy, like St. Francis, who was a thoroughly happy man precisely because he was poor in spirit. We have all noticed how those who are really poor for the sake of the kingdom seem to radiate a peculiar joy. From my own experience, I think I can say that the happiest people I have met were also the ones who lived their poverty most seriously. And it is noticeable also that they are the ones who share most readily. It is not that they give in order to make themselves important nor in a subconscious attempt to obligate others, but rather with the pure joy of unreservedly uniting themselves with others. Apostles not so much by what they say or do, but by what they are, they radiate the joy of the Good News, and this, after all, is the most effective of apostolic means.

In our affluent and consumer society we have to learn how to be poor. We live in a strange world! Where two-thirds of the world-population have barely enough to survive on, we have to make efforts to become poor. Unless we are specifically on our guard against the abuse, we shall find that things will flow into our rooms without our even noticing. All this is so natural! For many religious, so far as worldly goods were concerned, the day on which they took their vows was their nadir. The novitiate had fairly well stripped them of anything superfluous. But from this point onward, the progress seemed ever upward. Let us be honest: how many of us possess more today than when we took our vows? And of what we do have, how much do we really need? Is it not an implication of the vow that we should not have what we do not need? Here we must be realistic; we must consider honestly and fairly our physical, psychological, and spiritual needs. But then also we must consider just as honestly and fairly what we really do not need! I have noticed that religious who tamper with the ideal of poverty seem to lose to the same degree the happiness they once had. It seems that the more they have, the less contented they are, while at the same time they seem to lose apostolic effectiveness. When we indulge in a sort of possessiveness and mediocrity, a desire for comfort and security, or a concern for convenience, somehow we cause the salt to lose its savor and the gospel to lose its credibility. Evangelical poverty is not negative or lethargic; it is positive because of the exuberant life of the kingdom of God with which it is bursting. Where we allow this vitality of poverty to decrease, inevitably we experience a diminishing of the kingdom of God in us and around us.

As religious we would do well to remember that poverty is found at the very origin of religious life. Seventeen hundred years ago a young man in Egypt heard these gospel-words read by the priest during Mass: "If you wish to be perfect, go and sell what you own and give the money to the poor, and you will have treasure in heaven; then come, follow me" (Mt 19:21). With a sudden, compelling clarity he realized that the option was to be perfect or not; once the choice is made to be perfect, poverty is no longer optional. So he went home and immediately carried out the admonition he had heard. This man, Anthony, stands at the origin of the monks in the Egyptian desert and thus at the inception of all religious life. That the desert fathers had learned well the lesson of their master is seen in the delightful little story of Serapion, who sold his book of the gospels and gave the money to the poor, commenting wryly: "I have sold the book which told me to sell everything that I had and give it to the poor!"[1]

Happy the gentle they shall have the earth for their heritage! Evangelical gentleness is a fruit of the realization of God's love for me as I am. Once I am sure of God's acceptance, I can afford to be gentle because when God himself considers me worthwhile, there is no further need to assert myself. Since the certainty of God's infinite concern for me frees me from all self-concern, I can relate with people and accomplish my allotted tasks without needing to vaunt myself in them. As a result, a certain unselfishness comes about which makes my behavior serene and beneficent.

It can happen at times that an engine has too much inner friction and, consequently, develops a string of complications, eating up much energy—gasoline or electricity—and producing little. It makes a great deal of noise too, and it requires much cooling lest it become overheated. Finally, it wears out fast. There exist some people like this. They too have too much inner friction; there is too much self in their work, so that their compelling preoccupation becomes self and the opinion which others may have of them. They seem to have forgotten the admonitions of Christ: "Be careful not to parade your good deeds before men to attract their notice;. . .so when you give alms, do not have it trumpeted before you;. . .and when you pray do not imitate the hypocrites. . . ." (cf. Mt 6:1-5). These people consume much energy, yet accomplish relatively little. Moreover, they make a great fuss about the little they do, and require much patting on the back just to keep them going. All this is the exact opposite of the gentleness spoken of in the Beatitudes. The gentle of the gospel do not take themselves too seriously, and their healthy sense of humor prevents fanaticism. Because of their deep-seated conviction of God's love, they are able to view everything else as relative. Hence a certain equanimity in their attitudes and their manner, an equanimity which may easily lend itself to misinterpretation by the unwary. Here we have a striking example of the paradoxical in the gospel. The gentleness of the Beatitudes in no way means weakness; on the contrary, the gentle exhibit tremendous strength, a strength rooted in God himself.

Happy those who mourn: they shall be comforted. Perhaps in this Beatitude more than in any other we must seek beyond the surface for the true meaning of the words. To mourn, to lament—these are human reactions, and even a brief encounter with life will make all too apparent how omnipresent they are, how inescapable in our human situation. But that interpretation is too superficial. In this Beatitude we are dealing with a more basic, more penetrating reaction to human life, one that demands a more interior response. In his analysis of our reaction to human pain, Henri Nouwen has shown keen awareness of the layers of meaning involved in our response. To understand more fully the problem, we must first try to recognize the ambiguity that has developed around the very word *care*. Our understanding of the word can extend all the way from care as an implied threat (e.g., I will take care of him) to the rather commonplace expression of indifference and non-involvement (e.g., I don't care). In some instances it may even be implied that not to care is a more acceptable response than to care.

The word "care" finds its roots in the Gothic word *Kara*, which means mourning. The basic meaning of care, therefore, is to grieve, to experience sorrow, to cry out. In this fundamental meaning, there is no suggestion of condescension—the action of the strong toward the weak, the powerful toward the powerless. Rather, the man who cares enters deeply into the sorrow and pain of another before he attempts to do anything about it; i.e., his first reaction is necessarily a union of mind and heart before it seeks outward expression in action. Care, therefore, becomes a participation in the pain of another, a solidarity in suffering, and it is this sharing, this care, which must precede any attempt to lighten the burden. Cure without care is meaningless, an activity with no true human sentiment behind it. Perhaps our problem has been too great a preoccupation with curing to the detriment of truly caring. We busy ourselves in a variety of professional activities—all works of mercy, to be sure, but in themselves more concerned with the surface than with the depth. We use our expertise to change the painful realities of our suffering neighbor, but we forget that cure without care keeps us at a distance, unwilling or unable to share his burdens. Thus it can happen that cure can often become offensive rather than liberating—one reason, perhaps, why people in need often turn aside from proffered help. Not only individuals in need, but also oppressed minorities and even whole nations have declined help, preferring to suffer than to lose self-respect by accepting assistance from one who did not care.[2]

Happy those who hunger and thirst for what is right: they shall be satisfied. As parched soil thirsts for rain, these persons thirst for what God wills. As Jesus lived on the food of his Father's Will (Jn 4:34), these people long to see God's Will done in everything. Apart from this Will of God there exists no good, and they understand clearly that what God wants is always best. On the surface, God's Will may cause pain, but deep down it always gives peace and satisfaction. The sign that a person is truly led by God's Will is simply this: the fruits of the Spirit grow in him—love, joy, peace, patience, kindness, goodness, trustfulness, gentleness, and self-control (Gal 5:22). The criterion is not: does this person have the fruits of the Spirit or not? That would be a static approach which makes little sense. The touchstone is rather: is this person more joyful, more patient, more loving, more gentle...now than he used to be? Or more briefly, since being fully led by God's Will makes a man better, is this man becoming really good? There is a certain generosity required as a kind of pre-disposition for those truly seeking what is right. We can find that only when we set out with unconditional readiness to say yes to whatever is asked. If, on the contrary, we reserve acquiescence until after we have learned what that Will is demanding, we shall never know. Such reluctance is a certain sign that God is not God in our lives; something else has taken priority. It is only when we hunger and thirst for what is right that we can be filled with the good things of which Mary sang in her Magnificat (Lk 1:53).

Happy Are You

Happy the merciful; they shall have mercy shown them. In a way, mercy is the most hopeful of virtues. Time and again it offers to another the chance to make a new start, and far from locking him in his past, binding him securely to the evil he has done or the mistakes he has made, it offers the possibility of beginning again. Like love, mercy never despairs; it recalls always that there is more good in others than we realize. "There will be judgment without mercy for those who have not been merciful themselves; but the merciful need have no fear of judgment" (Jm 2:13). This is the constant doctrine of Christ, who wants us to forgive seventy times seven times (Mt 18:22) and who sets the spirit of forgiveness as the awesome norm in his prayer: "Forgive us our sins as we forgive those who sin against us" (Mt 6:12). It is the constant practice of Jesus also, which reaches its peak when he forgives his torturers at the very moment of their greatest cruelty and mercilessness (Lk 23:34). From this ultimate instance of Christ's loving mercy we learn more clearly how radical are the demands the spirit of forgiveness makes upon us; we must be ready to forgive not only those who admit they have done wrong and are ready to apologize for it, but we must go further and embrace even those who do not acknowledge their guilt. Moreover, our forgiveness is never merely a facile affair concerned only with the exterior because true mercy means that we must be willing to suffer from a person until our loving kindness may heal him. Forgiveness to this extent frees us of all resentment and gives us that peace which only Jesus can effect. In the last analysis, the merciful spoken of in the Beatitude is not so much a man who of himself is showing mercy, but rather one who has become, as it were, a transparency through whom the mercy of Christ can shine.

153

CALLED BY NAME

Happy the pure in heart: they shall see God. In the Old Testament it was impossible to see God and survive: "Man cannot see me and live," Yahweh says to Moses (Ex 33:20). And the New Testament seems at times to repeat this tenet: "God whose home is in inaccessible light, whom no man has seen and no man is able to see" (1 Tim 6:16). And yet, from Christ's words in this Beatitude we learn a further truth: the single-hearted can and will see God. To be single-hearted means to have no second motives. Such a heart seeks God alone. The vision of the single-hearted is direct, piercing through to the deepest Ground, which is God, and all creation becomes transparent, offering no obstruction to his eye. "The lamp of the body is the eye. It follows that if your eye is sound, your whole body will be filled with light" (Mt 6:22). I had always been struck by what seemed a direct opposition between the teaching of St. Ignatius and that of St. John of the Cross, both of whom lived in the sixteenth century and were what we now call Spaniards. St. Ignatius teaches ever so often that we can find God in everything. St. John repeats just as often that we must find God by way of *nada*, nothing. Whenever we find satisfaction in anything, be it ever so holy, we must give it up. When I first discovered this antithesis, I felt rather fortunate in being a disciple of St. Ignatius. But it did not take me long to discover that the two saints were teaching exactly the same thing. St. Ignatius is saying that one who seeks God and God alone will indeed find him everywhere; consequently Ignatius insists on mortification as a necessary condition for really seeking God alone. He has many strong statements on this! St. John teaches that through the *nada* we shall certainly find God. And both John and Ignatius are saying that this

154

Beatitude is indeed true: it is the man of single purpose, of pure heart who will find God.

Happy the peacemakers; they shall be called sons of God. To be a peacemaker is not easy, nor may it be a very 'in' thing. On the one hand, it may seem that my efforts to bring about peace are a plea for a compromise of principles, that I am trying to maintain the establishment in a society impatient for reform. On the other hand, it may be that even my efforts to bring about peace may cause estrangement and suffering from those for whom I am working. In spite of the difficulties, however, I must try, for to be a peacemaker is very much in line with the mission of Christ. He was announced by the prophet Isaiah as the "prince of peace," (Is 9:6), and at his birth the angels heralded him with the words, "Glory to God and peace to men." Christ does not merely *bring* glory to God and peace to men; he *is* it. "He is the peace between us" (Eph 2:14). In his priestly prayer at the end of his life Christ prays several times that all his followers may be one as he and his Father are one, setting this unity as a necessary condition whereby he will be believed (Jn 17:21-23). In spite of the urgency of his plea, however, the early Church had some difficulties with this. "What could be more unspiritual than your slogans, 'I am for Paul' and 'I am for Apollos'?" (1 Cor 3:4). In our time it may well be a special call and charism to seek out and preserve unity in diversity. Just as the community of Taizé from its beginning has sought for ecumenism amid the discord of the churches and by its striving for unity has found and radiated much inspiration and authenticity, so we, in the same way, should try in the pluriformity of faith-experience within the Catholic Church and its religious life to avoid destructive division and to stimulate unity to its depth. This demands that we truly eliminate all pettiness and hold ourselves ready to pay the price necessary for a deep foundation in Jesus Christ (cf. 1 Cor 3:11). Only in this way can we truly follow the Lord in being a peacemaker.

Happy those who are persecuted in the cause of right: theirs is the kingdom of heaven. We learn in this Beatitude that even persecution is part of our heritage. "You must not be surprised, brothers, when the world hates you" (1 Jn 3:13). If I am a partner of Christ I must share what happened to him. If I want to help build the kingdom of God on earth, I must follow the pattern set by Christ: "If the world hates you, remember that it hated me before you. If you belonged to the world, the world would love you as its own...A servant is not greater than his master" (Jn 15:18-20). To be persecuted in the cause of right brings us close to Jesus. At times it is a grace to be an outcast, to be looked down upon. Without experience of this, there is danger that we may be building not the kingdom of God, but our own kingdom. It is remarkable how persecutions can indeed establish the kingdom of God—a paradox that is amply illustrated throughout the crowded pages of history. One of the most beautiful witnesses to the active presence of this truth among us today is the prayer of Alexander Solzhenitsyn, forged of his experience of eight years in Soviet prisons and concentration camps. After having endured so many injustices, hardships, and cruelties, he is able to pray in this serene and peaceful way which I consider a splendid example of the Beatitude:

> How easy it is to live with you, O Lord.
> How easy to believe in You.

Happy Are You

When my spirit is overwhelmed within me,
When even the keenest see no further than the night,
And know not what to do tomorrow,
You bestow on me the certitude
That you exist and are mindful of me,
That all the paths of righteousness are not barred.

As I ascend into the hill of earthly glory,
I turn back and gaze, astonished, on the road
That led me here beyond despair,
Where I too may reflect Your radiance upon mankind.

All that I may yet reflect, You shall accord me,
And appoint others where I shall fail.[3]

Thirteen

BREAK AND SHARE

There are many ways of approaching the incidents in Christ's life which offer food for our lives—enlightenment, encouragement, consolation—but the more valuable way, probably, is to stand with Christ at the very center, trying to look upon the incidents of his life with the full sweep of his glance, to see not just the results, but more important-ly, the inspiration of his action; to contemplate not merely what he did, but how and why. This method will lead us most deeply into the heart of the gospel, and there at its innermost center we shall be able to understand more clearly the true meaning of Christian revelation: Christ was not a man who acted like God, nor a God who acted like man; he was God-made-man, the incarnate one who had come from his Father and who had only one purpose at heart—to show us the way to the Father. And he would accomplish this not by some transcendent action on our minds and wills, but by being present to us and serving us in our most human conditions—in hunger and thirst, in suffering and fear. The apostles had learned this lesson well, but only after much hesitation and many false starts. They had learned, however, and in the gospels they have set this message out clearly so that we too might understand. If we approach the gospels in this spirit, we shall be caught up into the cosmic scope of Christ's own mission, and we shall grasp more clearly the real meaning of any given incident in Christ's life. We shall see in it his constant preoccupation with the Father; we shall see that his Father's love for man was really the most precious truth he shared with us, and that when he seemed most concerned with the ordinary, humdrum needs of men, he was at the same time never losing sight of man's deeper need. It is contemplation of this kind which will lead us to achieve in our own life the interaction between contemplative prayer and apostolic mission which is our present concern.

Almost any event in the gospel, if approached in this spirit, will yield this fruit, but there are some incidents which are pivotal and their significance seems more vital. One such incident is the story of the feeding of five thousand persons who had followed Christ to hear his teaching, but who had become tired and hungry in the course of the lesson, and whose very human misery had appealed to the heart of Christ. All four evangelists recount the episode, and the three synoptics are all careful to point out that the incident had been preceded by a period of withdrawal, of quiet prayer (Mt 14:13-21; Mk 6:30-44; Lk 9:10-17; Jn 6:1-15). John places the event shortly before the Passover, i.e., before Christ's departure for Jerusalem, where a new and vital phase of his ministry is about to begin. It is entirely in keeping with all we know of Christ to see him preparing himself for the coming challenges by retiring into solitude for prayer. Luke tells us that "he would always go off to some place where he could be alone and pray" (5:16). And when the disciples in the first flush of excitement after their initial experiences in their mission came to Jesus filled with their accounts of what had happened, he quietly said, " 'You must come away to some lonely place all by yourselves and rest for a while'; for there were so many coming and going that the apostles had no time even to eat. So they went off in a boat to a lonely place where they could be by themselves" (Mk 6:31-33). Christ wanted to be sure that his apostles had understood this enduring need of all who are involved in ministering to men. What looks like an abrupt prescription, a pre-emptory command, is really evidence of the deep concern Christ felt for his disciples, who still had to learn that such withdrawal for prayer in solitude was not only advisable, but necessary.

To find rest with Jesus is beautiful, but it is not easy. There are so many ways in which we think we can find rest. We know that that deepest peace which the world cannot give is found only with Christ, and we think that we are willing to pursue this at any price—but then, we must be willing to pay the true price. It is not easy to become a man or woman of prayer, to achieve the proper balance between withdrawal and involvement, to see the one as a continuation of the other. The incident on the hillside of Galilee is a beautiful portrayal of this rhythm of prayer and work, for the account begins with the prayer of Christ, continues through the busy activity of feeding a huge throng and cleaning up after the meal, and concludes with the significant words of John: "Jesus. . .escaped back to the hills by himself."

As with all the important events in the life of Christ, the incident begins quietly, almost casually. Christ and his disciples had been alone, on the hillside, discoursing of the things of God, praying—and suddenly there they were, a huge crowd of men and women who had walked the long distance around the lake to listen further to the words of this Master who spoke so simply and so straightforwardly. In his reception of these people Jesus shows clearly how readily the transition from prayer to work can be made.

161

He showed neither officiousness nor annoyance in his manner with the crowd, but immediately, as Luke tells us with characteristic sensitiveness, he "made them welcome and talked to them about the kingdom of God" (9:11).

Mark carries us still deeper into the mind and heart of Christ at this crucial moment: "...Jesus took pity on them because they were like sheep without a shepherd, and he set himself to teach them at some length" (6:34). Like sheep without a shepherd—the very phrase evokes that image of Yahweh which is so constant in the Old Testament, one which Christ himself had used so frequently. It was not the fault of the poor and the little ones of Israel that they were so far from their God. Years before, the message had sounded through the words of the prophet Ezekiel:

> You have failed to make weak sheep strong, or to care for the sick ones, or bandage the wounded ones. You have failed to bring back strays or look for the lost. On the contrary, you have ruled them cruelly and violently. For lack of a shepherd they have scattered, to become the prey of any wild animal; they have scattered far (Ez 34:4-5).

But Yahweh will not abandon his sheep in their plight; he promises that he will send the right kind of shepherd, that in fact he himself will come to be that shepherd:

> The Lord Yahweh says this: I am going to look after my flock myself and keep all of it in view. As a shepherd keeps all his flock in view when he stands up in the middle of his scattered sheep, so shall I keep my sheep in view. I shall rescue them from wherever they have been scattered during the mist and darkness. I shall bring them out of the countries where they are; I shall gather them together from foreign countries and bring them back to their own land. I shall pasture them on the

mountains of Israel, in the ravines and in every inhabited place in the land. I shall feed them in good pasturage; the high mountains of Israel will be their grazing ground;. . .they will browse in rich pastures on the mountains of Israel. I myself will pasture my sheep. I myself will show them where to rest—it is the Lord Yahweh who speaks. I shall look for the lost one, bring back the stray, bandage the wounded and make the weak strong. I shall watch over the fat and healthy. I shall be a true shepherd to them (34:11-16).

We know how true a shepherd Christ was, even to laying down his life for his sheep. But there is more to the lesson than a description of what Christ did on a particular day and with a special group. The cry of Ezekiel is both warning and summons, and each of us who has been entrusted with a portion of Christ's flock must reflect deeply on its meaning for us. We know how innumerable are the sheep of Christ, but perhaps we do not always understand their hunger. Often they are seeking a pasture that is lost to them, and they need a shepherd to show them how and where to find it. They hunger often for the bread of Christ, but they are not always aware just what this bread is. They long for Christ, but their picture of him is distorted and unreal; they have been taught to think of God as an avenging God who will punish them mercilessly for their guilt, and it is against this God of vengeance that they rebel. How great is their need for a shepherd who will bring the true gospel to them! There are those too who do not want the ministrations of their shepherd, who close their heart to the truth and turn away from his care. Here above all, the shepherd has need of the patience, the endurance, the love which Christ has shown for his flock, and he must persevere in order to find entrance into their hearts lest they perish in misery and hunger.

163

CALLED BY NAME

Jesus climbed the hillside and sat down with his disciples. John, for whom the event had transcendent significance, tells us that it was shortly before the Passover, thus making a connection between this action and the later Paschal meal at which Christ once again used bread to feed his disciples, and once more, in the long discourse following the Supper presented the true meaning of his mission and of his Father's love.

Both on the hillside of Galilee and in the Paschal supper room Christ had used the most ordinary means for an extraordinary gift—he gave bread. But how meaningful was that simple gift! At Easter-time, associated as it was with the death and resurrection of Christ, the Bread of the Eucharist became still more significant, recalling as it was meant to do the death and the new life of Easter. Here on the hillside in Galilee Jesus was anticipating that gift of the Eucharist, and John understood profoundly the message. Of itself bread seems to signify well the meaning of life and of death. Bread comes from wheat, itself the fruit of a seed that has been put into the ground and has died. Moreover, the wheat can be used for making bread only after it has been sifted and crushed. In the hands of Christ this bread is used with God-like lavishness to appease the hunger of the multitude. As an image of our lives bread is thus a compelling figure. Burial in the ground, death, new life which yet must be pounded and kneaded, and finally full fruition in the hands of Christ—is not this the image of a Christian, of an apostle? To abandon ourselves to Christ means to place ourselves into his hands as bread to be broken by him. His hands are sensitive and tender, we know, because they have blessed and caressed little ones and have suffered the pain of piercing nails. He will not destroy us nor tear us asunder; rather he will break us

164

gently, with his own hands drawing out the fruitfulness, those hands which have healed and cured and forgiven and restored to life. It is in such surrender that there lie great peace and great merit. Long years after, when John was recounting this miracle of the loaves in Galilee, he did it in such a way that we might understand the deeper significance of this bread in the hands of Christ, and that we might see in it not merely a miraculous multiplication of food, but more importantly still, a call to look upon Christ at work with his flock, inviting us to share with him in his task. If truly we give ourselves into the hands of Christ, he will make of us bread broken and spent for the multitude.

When Jesus, looking up, saw the crowds, he said to Philip, "Where can we buy some bread for these people to eat?" Surely he must have said this with a smile, for he knew he was asking a question that had no answer. He was aware that there was no human solution; in fact, he was giving Philip an impossible mission, but even in this he was Jesus the teacher. The apostles had to learn that of themselves they could not build the kingdom of God, necessary as such a work was. Their awareness of their inadequacy, their helplessness in the face of even simple human difficulties was a necessary prelude to their apostolic fruitfulness, and Jesus was anxious to teach them—and us—that always he is the indispensable core of our activity: "cut off from me you can do nothing" (Jn 15:5). Once we are convinced of this, deep peace comes. As long as we rely on self, we shall always be tense, anxious. As soon as we acknowledge that of ourselves we can do nothing, we enter into the liberating sphere of the gospel and we experience true freedom. It is when we truly let go that God can act in us and through us. This was the lesson he wanted Philip to learn.

John continues: "He only said this to test Philip; he himself knew exactly what he was going to do." Philip, however, missed the point. He showed himself an alert business man, quickly calculating the needs: "Two hundred denarii would only buy enough to give them a small piece each." But he had forgotten—or possibly had not yet learned—that before God we do not calculate. Christ's attitude was always different. His trust in God's providence was complete (Mt 6:25-34). He saw his Father busy in everything: clothing the flowers of the field, feeding the birds in the sky, concerned always with the well-being of the world. Christ really lived surrounded by the gifts of his Father; he breathed them in like the air. As a consequence, he knew no concern, certainly no self-concern.

We are here brought face to face with one of the problems which in our day has exacted much honest soul-searching on the part of those who are anxious to understand truly the Christ-like response to the question of material goods. In how far can we literally accept the words of Christ and have no care for the material things of life? It is only through prayer that we can find the balance between an all too human reasonableness and a filial trust in God. St. Ignatius had a beautiful saying: We should work as hard as though everything depends on us and, at the same time, should trust as though everything depends on God. The whole point of his axiom is in the words: *at the same time.* The sign that I have found the right balance will be the lack of tension and of anxiety. Even in the face of difficulties we shall be at peace, for having surrendered to the Lord, we shall experience that detached and disinterested response that is the truly liberating gift of Christ and that proves most effective in the given circumstances. Christ's question to Philip about the supply of food was meant to lead him to a realization of this truth.

"One of his disciples, Andrew, Simon Peter's brother, said, 'There is a small boy here with five barley loaves and two fish; but what is that between so many?' " Knowing how utterly inadequate the supply is, the apostle seems almost ashamed to offer it. Here again we have an instance of Christ showing his disciples what is meant by true stewardship. It is not that Andrew's offering is adequate; were the people to depend on it alone, their problem would be insoluble. It is rather the totality of the offering, the generous giving of the whole which Christ can use and of which he can make a meal for the hungering. Once again we are reminded of the Eucharistic overtones of this gospel incident, which teaches that total giving, in a sense, is like a Eucharistic celebration in which we give all we have and then receive in return a piece of bread, but bread that has become infinitely more than all we gave, for it is now the Body of Christ. Both here and later in Jerusalem we see Christ giving to his flock the bread which remains a lasting proof of his *emeth*, his fidelity in loving concern, but in Galilee the bread was merely a harbinger of the tremendous reality still to come.

"Then Jesus took the loaves, gave thanks, and gave them out to all who were sitting ready; he then did the same with the fish, giving out as much as was wanted." Christ's first act was to return thanks for the food they were about to receive. It is a significant act, one we should never forget or pass over too lightly. Some years ago, at the time when *Honest to God* was creating such a stir, a priest one day remarked with assurance that Christ never really prayed in the gospel. He might have taken some time preparing himself for things to come, it is true, but he never took time out to pray. This is probably one of the most appalling remarks ever made by one who should have known better. It has been helpful, however, for I think I have never since read a gospel incident in which Christ is praying that I have not noted it especially. The truth is that Christ prays often, but so often and so naturally that we may easily overlook the fact. For him prayer is like the atmosphere in which he lives, so much so that it is almost the last thing we notice. Here on the hillside, standing with the loaves of bread in his hands, offering thanks to the Father, Christ has become the host at the family feast and in this role he leads his family in giving thanks to the Father. Then he shares the food.

At this point Matthew adds a significant detail: "And breaking the loaves he handed them to his disciples who gave them to the crowds" (14:19)—a hint that helps us to understand the meaning of apostolate with and for Christ. Christ breaks the loaves and works the miracle, but he distributes it through men. Normally Christ's miracles will reach men only in this way. The light of God's lamp burns with the oil of our lives. This is the aspect of apostolic activity which raises it immediately into the realm of prayer. God needs us just as he needs the grain of wheat for the Eucharist. We too are to be broken, to be distributed, to be eaten. In this way we become part of the miracle; it is worked through us—but then, we have to be broken and distributed.

John tells us that Christ gave them "as much as they wanted." Even in his royal munificence Christ respects the freedom of man. He gave as much as they wanted; not more, for he would not force them; not less, for he would not deprive them. It is not God but we ourselves who set the limit. It is well to consider: do we ask enough from

God or are we too petty? Even modern psychiatry can tell us how tragic "too little" can be in our lives. A human potential, held down to the merely normal and the average when it is capable of a far greater reach, will experience only frustration and debility that will eventuate in neurosis just as surely as will the discontent and the self-mistrust of those who are striving ceaselessly to over-achieve. What is true in our psychological life can be even more true in our spiritual life, with effects that are more devastating. In this matter Ann Wylder has written:

> Many complex reasons have been documented for our experience of ennui, discontent and inauthenticity; but I suggest that one reason is that we did not dare to aspire to mysticism, by which I mean the finding, the faith-discovery, of God in all reality.[1]

Do we really want this discovery of God? Is it truly our ideal? In Galilee the hungry ones received what they wanted. There is danger always that we are not really serious, that we are merely romantic in our aspirations.

When they had eaten enough, Christ said to the disciples, " 'Pick up the pieces left over, so that nothing gets wasted.' So they picked them up and filled twelve hampers with scraps left over from the meal of five barley loaves." Here again we see something of the deeper meaning of this miracle. It is not so much that the crowd is satisfied, but that in their satiety we see the abundance of God's giving and recognize Jesus as the fullness of God. Like the miracle at Cana, this multiplication of the loaves refers to the Eucharist; both miracles show Christ producing in abundance, a tremendous amount of bread and wine, signs of that Eucharistic banquet we are still living on, the daily proof of his limitless love and his care.

On that evening in Galilee Jesus wanted to do so much more than merely satisfy the hunger of men's bodies, yet men were not yet ready to understand the full import of his message. Mark says, "They were utterly and completely dumbfounded, because they had not seen what the miracle of the loaves meant; their minds were closed" (6:52). And John lets us see what their blindness led to: "The people seeing this sign that he had given, said 'This really is the prophet who is to come into the world.' . . .Jesus, could see they were about to come and take him by force and make him king. . . ." This type of kingship was far short of what Jesus had really meant. Later in the same chapter of John we read of his further attempt to help men understand: "I tell you most solemnly, you are not looking for me because you have seen the signs but because you had all the bread you wanted to eat." They had had the bread, but they had missed its meaning, so he added: "Do not work for food that cannot last, but work for food that endures to eternal life, the kind of food the Son of Man is offering you. . .' Then they said to him, 'What must we do if we are to do the works that God wants?' " The answer here is all-important: "This is working for God: you must believe in the one he has sent" (Jn 6:26-29).

This, then, is the final answer for an apostle: he must believe in Christ; this is all that really counts. He must work in such a way that his whole task is filled with that faith in Christ and, in fact, becomes an expression of his faith. Too easily our work can be an idol, blocking our faith because in it we tend to rely on ourselves, or debasing our service by turning it into an effort merely to oblige others, or even making of it a status or a career. Then it is

170

no longer faith that is operative; it is we alone who are achieving the task. It is no longer the people whom we serve; rather, we really abuse the people in order to serve ourselves. The miracle of the loaves is the sign of the contrary. It is belief in Christ and surrender to him which are important. The outcome of our work is secondary to this; in fact, it may even be a hindrance. Christ has shown us what to do when the people are enthusiastic about us and fall in love with us and want to make us a king. He left them, escaping back into the hills, alone with his Father from whom all good things come.

Fourteen

LAST WORDS

We shall probably never become accustomed to the awesome finality of death nor accept lightly the sudden silence which follows the last shallow breath marking the end. We find ourselves repeating the last words spoken by the dying person, combing them once more for meaning, as though by prolonging his words we could in some way prolong his life. We listen more intently to those words too, for the mystery which surrounds any death seems to lend special value to last words, enhancing them with a depth of meaning we are anxious to sound. This reaction is true at any deathbed, probably, for it is a normal human experience. When the dying person is beloved, however, our impulse to gather up his last words is all the greater. Dreading the silence to follow, we try to fill it with the parting observations of one we have loved.

In this spirit we ponder the words spoken by Christ during the agonizing hours on Golgotha. It is not that the lessons from the cross are new. There is still the same concern for the ravages of guilt in the hearts of men he had come to save, the same attention to the needs of others, the same awareness of the work entrusted to him by his Father, above all, the same surrender to the Will of the Father even in the throes of death. And yet because these messages are uttered so shortly before death, we recognize in them a kind of summation of all that has gone before. When prayerfully, attentively, we read the words of the dying Christ, we experience the urgency of each separate "word," reaffirming as it does the meaning of Christ in our own lives and in the lives of all men.

Father, forgive them; they do not know what they are doing (Lk 23:34).

Father, forgive—it is altogether what we would expect, that the very first words of the dying Christ should be addressed to his Father. No other love, no other concern had surpassed his preoccupation with his Father; to find him turning to his Father at this time, therefore, seems right. And yet, there is more to it than that. It is for forgiveness that Jesus is praying here. It would be hard to devise a greater contrast than that offered by the words of Christ and the setting in which they were uttered. St. Luke, after repeating Christ's plea, "Father, forgive them; they do not know what they are doing," adds immediately "then they cast lots to share out his clothing." The contrast between the two sentences serves only to emphasize more starkly the utter callousness of the executioners and to make more clear how appalling was the scene of Christ's death. There was not only the physical agony of the crucifixion, which in itself should have been sufficiently brutal to impress even his enemies. Beyond this suffering, however, there was the harsh, unfeeling reaction of the leaders of Israel, who saw in the crucified teacher of Nazareth a religious and political victory over which they gloated. Crowding in triumph about the cross, they did not allow him even that privacy which men instinctively grant to one near death. On Calvary there was no respect for his human agony; there was no mercy. Having achieved their end, these men took a certain complacency in their accomplishment, mocking him, taunting him, boasting of

174

their success in having exposed his lying claims to be God's own Son. It is hard to imagine that man can be so sadistic towards a fellow-man.

Inevitably the thought occurs: how could men act thus? Or the more searching question: how could God allow this to happen? We find it hard to imagine ourselves in Christ's place, hanging there in agony on the tree of shame, yet to do so would help us to measure more accurately the distance between an all too human reaction and the response of Christ, who had come to teach us his way to the Father. We would certainly have cried out against this cruel mob, possibly even have cursed them in our hearts, and God as well. Perhaps with the last burst of energy we might have formed a fist with our hands pierced with nails and have poured out our anger and frustration on men who could be so savage. But Christ does none of these things. He does not come down from the cross as he is taunted to do. That might have been our response, crushing our enemies by obvious power, forcing them by the miracle to admit that we really were the Son of God. But that is not Christ's way. Jesus convinces not by crushing, but by forgiving. He vindicates his divine mission not by coming down from the cross, but by staying there, by forgiving even malice such as this.

"They do not know what they are doing." We catch here a glimpse of the vast difference between the kingdom of God and our kingdom. Jesus is so inscrutably different. I would want to scream out in protest, to say that it is not true that they do not know what they are doing. For months they have been scheming, setting up their plans meticulously, hiring a traitor, working out the details of the capture. Indeed, they know very well what they are doing. And yet, Jesus is right. On the organizational level they know; but on a deeper level they do not. Theirs has been the way of refusal: they have never understood who Christ really is, have never grasped his mission nor opened their hearts to the love of God embodied in Christ. And because they have never let Christ's love enter, they have never really known him. From these words of the dying Jesus I can understand who he really is; I can fathom the depth of his love which is not turned away even from those who scorn him as he dies, mocking him cruelly. They may persist, with no sign of repentance or of sorrow; they may even exult in their achievement. And yet he forgives, offering in this gesture of clemency a last effort to help them understand something of his love.

It is not only the boisterous crowd on Calvary which needs God's forgiveness, however. In the words of Christ I too can grasp a little of what it means to be saved, and understand how I need this word of forgiveness which he will have to speak over my life again and again. Because these are the words of a dying master, inevitably they recall his other words on the same subject. In the prayer he taught us to say to the Father he gave us the measure of our spirit of forgiveness, and from these words on the cross I realize what a dangerous prayer this is. I recall how he has taught that our forgiveness must be patient and unwearying: we are to forgive our neighbor seventy times seven times, and it is to be a forgiveness that extends to all kinds of wrongs, the great as well as the trivial. The parable of the intolerant servant (Mt 18:23-35) who had been forgiven the deliberately fantastic debt of nine million dollars but had refused to pardon another for a debt of fifteen dollars underscores how vast is the difference between what God pardons us and what we are called upon to forgive in our neighbor. Here on Calvary as I listen to the dying Christ, I am brought to a moment of truth and I ask myself: do I really forgive? Have I ever in my whole life really forgiven? Are there hard feelings in me for anyone? In superficial matters there is little difficulty; these I can pardon quite readily. But when I am hurt in my deepest feelings, forgiveness is another, far more difficult question. The wounds inflicted by others, especially by those from whom we have a right to expect more—for example, those in authority—can be so deep and so painful that of ourselves we are incapable of truly forgiving. And where the hurt is particularly deep, we need the healing of Christ. The tragedy of unforgiving is corrosive. It is possible to meet people who for years have carried bitter feelings in their hearts so that they have, in a sense, become warped, and the bitterness has become part of them. At such times there is only one thing to do: to go to the cross and stand there still for a long time, just watching Jesus as he dies. It is there that the trauma will be healed, and we shall be able to forgive. Luke says, ". . .power came out of him that cured them all," (6:19), and John adds, "And when I am lifted up from the earth, I shall draw all men to myself" (12:32). When Christ is dying, the healing strength that flows from him reaches its peak. We must expose our wound to this healing power of the dying Lord; then we shall be able to forgive. This may take time; bitterness may depart only slowly, but it has to go if truly we are to be followers of Christ.

Today you will be with me in paradise (Lk 23:43).

The second word of Christ on the cross presents a brief dramatic interlude which by its very simplicity thrills and encourages us. There, swirling about the suffering Christ is an ocean of hatred, and on the cross next to him a

177

criminal looks down in wonder on the scene. He sees them all: the Pharisees, the scribes, religious leaders whose fanaticism has led them in their rage to this moment of vengeance. All fanaticism is dangerous because it entails a mindless insistence that can achieve no lasting good. Religious fanaticism is worst of all, and its long, sorry history reveals all too clearly the excesses to which its blind fury can lead as those who, caught in its grip, "with God on their side," brutally steamroll any who get in their way. The appalling thing is that they can find joy in the pain they are inflicting. It is this sense of satisfaction on the face of the enemies of Christ which strikes the dying thief, a sense of joy in what they are doing—and the man can tell it from their expressions. He hears the clamor of hatred coming from their mouths, those mouths which should have been preaching God's love. And then from the mouth of the one who like him is dying the death of a criminal he hears the pleading words, "Father, forgive them." In the contrast this dying man realizes that the one next to him, this battered, ravaged man, is more than just a human being. In that moment of light he pierces the mist, sees something of the divine in Jesus, for no one could react against so much hatred in such a gentle way if divine power were not in him. Impulsively he breaks out in prayer: "Jesus, remember me when you come into your kingdom." And by the word of the dying Jesus the criminal is transformed instantly into a saint.

"The word of God is something alive and active" (Heb 4:12). It is powerful, and when it is uttered, something happens. Here on Calvary we see the strength of the word of God, its power: "Today you will be with me in paradise." Not tomorrow, but today, because a man who can pray like that, who can encounter Christ in this way, that man is ready for the kingdom of God.

Jesus said to his mother, 'Woman, this is your son.' Then to the disciple he said, 'This is your mother.' And from that moment the disciple made a place for her in his home (Jn 19:26-27).

At Cana Jesus had said, "Woman, why turn to me; my hour has not yet come" (Jn 2:4). Now the hour has come, and the mother will share it with her son. When at the annunciation Mary had spoken her *fiat*, she had no means of knowing the implications of that assent. Christ has been a surprise to her ever so often, a surprise that at times was a tremendous joy, but he has also been a surprise of bitterness and suffering. Mary had known that both the joy and the suffering turned out to be blessings, that everything shared with Christ is a grace. Here on the hill of the crucifixion she is encountering the most far-reaching of her challenges, one that she could never have anticipated in that *fiat* of Nazareth. Yet here there is no change. As she has done throughout her life, she answers simply, "Let this too be done." And now Christ gives her away. "Woman, this is your son...this is your mother." No name is mentioned here because the meaning is so vast, extending to every disciple standing beneath the cross. In the plan of his Father Mary's divine maternity is not enough; she must become the mother of each of us. If we are to grow in the likeness of Christ—and that is our only purpose (Rom 8:29), then it is Mary who must be Christ's mother in us too. Like so many of Christ's words, these have their roots in the distant past and their import will last forever. "This is your mother," the woman we have been awaiting since that momentous prophecy in Eden:

CALLED BY NAME

I will make you enemies of each other:
you and the woman,
your offspring and her offspring.
It will crush your head
and you will strike its heel (Gen 3:15).

In the death and resurrection of Christ Satan is indeed crushed, but the full application of that victory will be seen only in the life of the Church as it confronts the evil of Satan in the ages still to come. Here too Mary's role is vital: through her bond with Christ, she is still a life-giving mother, an image of the Church which perpetuates for us always the life of Christ among men.

My God, my God, why have you deserted me? (Mt 27:47).
This word opens an abyss of suffering. Throughout his life Christ has found his strength, his food in the Will of his Father. Through all the stages of his suffering, which he could manage because he knew the Father's favor rested upon him, even in Gethsemane, he could still murmur: "Your will be done, not mine." But now the awareness of his Father's presence has left him. He is truly stripped. They had taken away his clothes, the only material possessions he had had. They had taken away his good name and had slandered him. His friends had run away, leaving him in terrible loneliness. He has given away his mother, and now his Father is also taken away from him. Nothing is left except complete loneliness, utter desertion. Closed in by desolation as by a wall, there is no perspective left for him; abandoned by all, he has no one to whom to turn. The dryness of our prayer is so tiny compared to the desolation of Christ here. Once more, however, we are brought face to face with the paradox of Christ, for in his

words we learn how he manages to turn even bitter desolation into prayer. When he seems utterly crushed, with no words of his own to express his sufferings, he has recourse to a psalm made meaningful by a tradition of centuries. There is a secret of the psalms: they can transform even deepest desolation into prayer, and this by no miraculous formula but by a very human response. In them there is no fast, easy-going resignation; there people fight and struggle and despair; they curse and complain. But even while doing all this, they present it to God, telling the whole of their struggle to him. In this way they transform their human feelings into prayer. They are like the stream of living water gushing from under the temple threshold (Ez 47:1) which never stops flowing. We should learn to let ourselves be taken up into that stream. When I pray a psalm, I am part of that immense body of people of both the Old and the New Testament who have prayed this way. The people I admire, the saints I venerate, Jesus himself, have all prayed these psalms; in praying them I am united with them all.

The agony of Calvary was turned into a prayer in the words of the psalm that Christ quoted. His sufferings were now taken up into the sufferings of those many generations who had learned to pray that way. But there is an added significance, for in Psalm 22, as in so many others, the complaints and the rebellion against God are turned into resignation and eventually into triumph. This subtle resolution was not lost upon the men standing beneath the cross, listening to the cry of Jesus. Scribes and Pharisees as they were, they knew well the scriptures, knew them by heart—in fact, could reconstruct a whole psalm if they heard a single fragment. In quoting this one line, therefore,

CALLED BY NAME

Christ had implicitly quoted the entire psalm, including the invincible trust of its conclusion:

Then I shall proclaim your name to my brothers.
Praise you in full assembly:
you who fear Yahweh, praise him!
Entire race of Jacob, glorify him!
Entire race of Israel, revere him!

For he has not despised
or disdained the poor man in his poverty,
has not hidden his face from him,
but has answered him when he called.

You are the theme of my praise in the Great Assembly,
I perform my vows in the presence of those who fear
        him.

The whole earth, from end to end, will remember and
        come back to Yahweh;
all the families of the nations will bow down before him.
For Yahweh reigns, the ruler of nations!
Before him all the prosperous of the earth will bow
        down,
before him will bow all who go down to the dust.
And my soul will live for him, my children will serve
        him;
men will proclaim the Lord to generations still to come,
his righteousness to a people yet unborn. All this he has
        done.

Actually, Psalm 22 can be divided into three parts, the first two of which express utter desolation. The third part, however, is an exultant paean to the God who will save his people. We would do wrong to understand Christ's words only as a cry of suffering, therefore, without hearing also his triumph. Certainly the Pharisees understood this; they recognized his words for what they were: a cry of victory, of confidence in his Father.

I am thirsty (Jn 19:28).

Certainly on Calvary there was enough to make Christ thirsty: loss of blood, open wounds exposed to the scorching sun of mid-day, fever from his wounds. As the psalms say: "In my thirst they gave me vinegar to drink" (Ps 69:21), and "My palate is drier than a potsherd and my tongue is stuck to my jaw" (Ps 22:16). It makes sense that he is thirsty—and yet if his listeners understand his thirst only in a physical sense, they have missed the depths of this word. Behind the dreadful thirst for water, in fact behind the entire passion of Jesus, the driving force is actually his thirst for men, his thirst for me. Christ himself this dying Christ consumed with a parching thirst, is an invitation to draw from the source of living water:

> Oh, come to the water all you who are thirsty,
> though you have no money, come! (Is 55:1).

It is Christ in his death who will give us this living water. At the height of the last Feast of the Tabernacles which Jesus celebrated, while the liturgical ceremonies centered on the living water which the priests drew from the well of Siloam and offered in libation on the temple square, Jesus had applied the prophecy of Isaiah to himself: "If any man is thirsty, let him come to me! Let the man come and drink who believes in me. As scripture says: From his breast [i.e., from Jesus himself, according to the oldest tradition] shall flow fountains of living water."   Then

John adds for those who would not understand: "He was speaking of the Spirit which those who believed in him were to receive; for there was no Spirit as yet because Jesus had not yet been glorified" (Jn 7:37-39). This is what he has promised. Indeed, the dying, thirsting Jesus will give us the Holy Spirit, will inspire us if only we take time quietly, silently to contemplate him in his agony on the cross until he gives up his spirit and until we see together with his blood the water flowing from his pierced side. Then we shall be filled with his Spirit, and indeed from his thirst we can quench our own.

It is accomplished (Jn 19:30).

What the prophets had foretold is accomplished. Everything has been realized: his thirty years of hidden life, his three years of public life, his three days of passion, his three hours of agony—and in everything he has glorified his Father. Now he is burned out. It is time for the Father to take over:

> I have glorified you on earth
> and finished the work
> that you gave me to do.
> Now, Father, it is time for you to glorify me
> with that glory I had with you
> before ever the world was (Jn 17:4-5).

Here again I learn from these last words of Christ that the words "glory" and "glorification" have a very special meaning in the gospel, one wholly unlike the superficial meaning so often attributed to them. In the gospel glory comes through the cross and through death. The grain of wheat must die in order to bear fruit. If I am to realize something of the kingdom of God I must go by way of the cross; there is no other way to glory, to a fruitful apostolate. It is not that God wants us to suffer. On the contrary, he wants us to live and not to die. He wants us to laugh and not to weep. In the human predicament, however, what God wants can only materialize through suffering. Evil in this world can be overcome only with pain. But God himself guarantees that if we fight the way God wants us to, the victory will be ours and God's kingdom will come about. May this word of my dying Lord give me the strength to accomplish this mission of mine, as Christ has accomplished his, by fulfilling everything the Father wants us to do.

When Jesus had cried out in a loud voice, he said, 'Father, into your hands I commit my spirit.' With these words he breathed his last (Lk 23:46).

These last spoken words of the dying Jesus are probably the most beautiful of all. He ends as he had begun, speaking directly to his Father. More than from all the other words, I can learn so much from this one. I can repeat this prayer of Christ in all circumstances: when I am anxious, upset, fearful, weighed down with scruples, feeling at a loss, hurt, lonesome, I can always safely commit my spirit into the Father's hands. Abandonment into his Father's hands has been the keyword for the whole life of Christ. He could have no other in its consummation. This word has been strikingly portrayed by a German artist in his picture of two human hands holding gently, yet strongly, a little bird. These are God's hands holding me (Ps 139:10). Once I am there, I am absolutely safe; "there is no snatching out of my Father's hand" (Jn 10:29 NAB). This is coming home!

185

Fifteen

THE HOUR HAS COME

Christ is the center of human history. This is literally so true that we reckon all the actions of man in the long, turbulent years of his existence as having taken place before Christ or after him. More relevant than the matter of dates, of course, is the fact that no human life has ever had such impact on the history of mankind as Jesus has had, an impact which constitutes him truly center.

But his life has had its own center, its pivotal point around which the whole thrust of the mystery of Christ revolves. This is found in his passing, the paschal mystery with its two-fold aspect of death and resurrection which together form the central mystery of Christ. This passing of Christ is the center, the heart of his life and, consequently, the heart of the history of mankind. It is not so strange that this event resounded through the cosmos. At the moment of his death, we are told, the earth quaked, rocks were split, tombs were opened, the sun was eclipsed, the veil of the temple was torn in two from top to bottom, Satan fell like lightning from heaven, the very cosmos was shaken to its depth. The event had been foreshadowed in many of the major events of the Old Testament: the sacrifice of Isaac, the paschal lamb, the exodus through the Red Sea, but all of these were only anticipating types of what is taking place on Calvary. Right now, exegetes figure that the actual event took place on Friday, April 7, in the year 30.

He hangs there outstretched above an earth which has repulsed and rejected him so that he no longer belongs to this world. At the same time he is outstretched beneath a heaven which is grey, threatening, completely closed, and on this barred firmament the "No" of God to sin is clearly written. Christ hangs between these two realities, earth and heaven, but he belongs to neither—yet in his very expulsion he is the link binding them together.

His eyes are bloodshot; his temples feverish; he is defenseless against the torment of flies, mosquitoes, hornets. Held firmly by the nails, he cannot move. There is the rasping breath, the tremendous exhaustion, the stifling, suffocating agony. All this was part of his physical pain, and it was very real. Yet this suffering was intensified by the obvious satisfaction which his enemies were finding in the event. The Pharisees are there for sure, gloating over their success, unwilling to miss one moment of the spectacle:

> A herd of bulls surrounds me,
> strong bulls of Bashan close in on me;
> their jaws are agape for me,
> like lions tearing and roaring (Ps 22:12-13).

They will not go away, these pious people, to let him die in peace, for they are convinced that by killing this man they are pleasing God. Hence he is a spectacle in which they find cause for complacency. There is no doubt about the satisfaction they are experiencing. These religious leaders of Israel are numerous, but their very presence makes Christ all the more lonely because it is so filled with hatred, so lacking in any sign of respect for his agony. The closer Jesus comes to death, the smaller becomes the circle of friends around him; eventually he ends alone. On Palm Sunday there had been quite a crowd, the gospel tells us, who had acclaimed Jesus. At the Last Supper there had been twelve at the beginning of the meal, eleven at its close. In Gethsemane there had been only three, and even these three, when they found his prayer too long, had slept. At Gethsemane's end there were none: "Then all the disciples deserted him and ran away" (Mt 26:56). Now on Calvary he is experiencing the utter loneliness of total abandonment; he no longer belongs to this earth, for he has been repulsed. It makes sense that Christ has to undergo in complete loneliness this death in which he cements his solidarity with us, for the more universal the meaning of a deed, the more lonely is its accomplishment. But why was this privacy not granted to him with respect and sympathy? Why this isolation and hatred?

Moreover, in this hour Christ no longer belongs to heaven either, for God too has deserted him: "My God, my God, why have you deserted me?" (Mt 27:46). St. Paul has expressed a little of the root of this anguish in what is probably the most cruel text of scripture: "For our sake God made the sinless one into sin" (2 Cor 5:21). He has taken on himself our sin completely, and while carrying the guilt of us all, has really become one with us. Such identification is possible when one truly loves, but the man who in his love experiences the guilt of his beloved as his own suffers intensely. It is because Christ loves us so greatly that our guilt has become his guilt and he has become sin. That on which his whole life was based, the love of his Father, has vanished, or at least, he experiences nothing of it in his dereliction. If we are to understand a little of Christ's dying agony, we must see this abandonment, this isolation not only from earth but also from

189

heaven as it truly affected him: Christ died in utter loneliness.

In this abandonment as in every other moment of his life it is Christ the savior whom we encounter. We seldom realize that our loneliness can be an invitation to share in the loneliness of Christ. In fact, it is very difficult to discover any sense at all in loneliness, let alone this profound call to participate in the agony of Christ. Yet it is precisely as a sharing of the dereliction of Jesus that our own loneliness can avoid self-pity and bitterness and can be transformed into fruitfulness.

We must remember that the suffering of his loneliness was intense. To be deserted by the Father who alone was the center of his life and thought was an agony before which even the courage of Christ shrank. Looking upon this suffering, we are tempted to wonder why the Father does not interfere, to ask how he can let his Son die such a cruel death without any intervention from that mercy and faithfulness which Christ has taught us to see in him. This is beyond our understanding because God's love is far greater than we can ever comprehend. The Father's love for Christ is here all right, but it is a super-love, a super-faithfulness which our human vision cannot encompass, and we can only watch in bewilderment as the Father permits the suffering of his Son to go on to the very end.

The eye of faith, not of our intellect, tells us that in all this the Father does remain faithful to his beloved Son, that indeed this very faithfulness has a divine dimension which will be shown most clearly in the resurrection to come. Even in his death, however, Jesus was still with the Father, sustained by that divine love which we cannot grasp. Christ's last words prove that he understood, for it was to his beloved Father that he entrusted himself, and with these words of confident abandonment he breathed his last. Those who knew scripture had already inferred this from Psalm 22, the first line of which Jesus had cried out on his cross; they knew that the conclusion of that psalm was a hymn of praise and confidence,—and they understood.

The death of a person always has a subduing influence on those who witness it. In the quiet which follows upon the death of Christ let us simply, with deep honesty, contemplate this death which, like the life it closed, was an act of total love. As we watch the death of Jesus, let us try to fathom somewhat its message. One of the first, overpowering lessons of Calvary is that it brings home to us the answer to that vital question of who we really are. The riddle of human identity has long haunted the hearts of men, and both pagans and Christians alike have set themselves to probe its mystery. "Know thyself!" the Oracle at Delphi had cautioned, since it supposed that such knowledge could provide a sustaining basis for human action. With the deeper, more humble insight of the believer, St. Augustine prayed: *"Noverim te, noverim me!*—that I may know you, that I may know myself!" Self-knowledge has always been recognized as important, perhaps at no time more so than in our own day. There are those who go as far as psycho-analysis to discover who they are. Others undertake sensitivity training or T-groups to find out how they come across to their associates. Psychiatrists attempt to lead an identity crisis back to the first years of life, even to the first months. But perhaps this is not far enough. Perhaps they should go still further back to the time before conception—and this is where the psychiatrists will fail, for they cannot know the whole. The real roots of life go far beyond birth or conception.

191

This is what we learn from the death of Christ, in which we can see how precious we are in the eyes of God. Now we can know who we are; namely, those dear to God, loved by him. That is the essence of our being: God's love has brooded over us, has created us, has held us in existence, has even given his Son that we may live:

> It is not easy to die even for a good man—though of course for someone really worthy, a man might be prepared to die—but what proves that God loves us is that Christ died for us while we were still sinners (Rom 5:7-8).

John had no other theme than this:

> God's love for us was revealed
> when God sent into the world his only Son
> so that we could have life through him;
> this is the love I mean:
> not our love for God,
> but God's love for us when he sent his Son
> to be the sacrifice that takes our sins away (1 Jn 4:9-10).

Here before the dead Christ, as this realization grows, we can ask the grace of that true self-knowledge which will banish once and for all any identity crisis. Here we can see how truly we are loved; we can see the price God has paid for us and thus can understand a little of what our worth is in the eyes of God.

Because his death is the ultimate proof of his love, we can be utterly convinced that no matter what may happen, we are secure in the love of Christ. For Paul this message was the basis of all his confidence:

Since God did not spare his own Son, but gave him up to benefit us all, we may be certain, after such a gift, that he will not refuse anything he can give (Rom 8:32).

For I am certain of this: neither death nor life, no angel, no prince, nothing that exists, nothing still to come, not any power, or height or depth, nor any created thing, can ever come between us and the love of God made visible in Christ Jesus our Lord (Rom 8:38-39).

Having been convinced of this overwhelming truth, we can understand better how we must bring knowledge of it to others. This apostolic dimension of the lesson of Calvary is inescapable. Beneath every crucifix belongs a globe, and it is to the men in every quarter of this globe that the message of Calvary must be carried. The early disciples, recognizing the universality of the redemption, tried insistently to convey their sense of wonder at the transforming effect of God's concern for men.

We too can learn from the death of Christ the value of other people. Perhaps this is what a truly Christian relationship is: to look upon each person as one redeemed by Christ. This is the most basic truth we can know about another, and on this we can build our common interests and concerns. We recognize the personal value of another because the Son of God died for him, and he has infinite value in the eyes of God the Father. Consequently, we must treat him with genuine respect and love, never reducing his immeasurable worth to the limited scope of what we know about him. If we relate to each other in this way, then undoubtedly we shall become apostles, and our approach to men will transmit something of the mystery of God's redeeming love which we acknowledge in each one. In this way we shall lead others to discover that the source of all value in life is to be found here in the crucified Christ of Golgotha.

It is not only the influence on others which the crucifixion of Christ effects, however, for the vital question always remains: what is its impact on me? In the *Spiritual Exercises* St. Ignatius proposes three questions which will help me to achieve the proper focus. He suggests that before my crucified Lord I ask: What have I done for Christ? What am I doing? What am I going to do? In other words, it is not the exuberance of feelings, not the emotional reactions which are important. More fundamentally, I must consider: Does the message of Christ's death really affect my life or does it remain a sounding brass? The disciple is no more than his master. If we are sincere, we must be prepared to share in his difficulties: "You are well aware, then, that anybody who tries to live in devotion to Christ is certain to be attacked" (2 Tim 3:12). If it happened to him, it will happen to us as well. The list of those who, undaunted by the trials of the way, have said "Yes" stretches far: Paul of Tarsus, Athanasius, John of the Cross, Mary Ward, Margaret Mary Alacoque, Alphonsus de Liguori, Lorenzo Ricci, Teilhard de Chardin—there is no age, no country, which has not produced its rota of dedicated Christians who have been tempered in genuine suffering, and the bewildering question always rises to plague us: Why were these men and women so afflicted? There is even the further question, paradoxical and possibly even scandalous: How does it happen that the ones inflicting the suffering were so often good, pious people, persons who, apparently, were also friends of God and on his side? Inevitably there follows the last query: On whose side is God? There is no easy answer for such questions; they involve the mystery of human limitations in affairs of God. One thing is certain—and the lesson of Calvary is incontrovertible here—God is not found where there is pressure or threat or contempt. God always respects and loves each of us, and invariably the fruits of his Spirit are evident: gentleness, patience, recollectedness. I know then, as I seek the answers to the questions of St. Ignatius, what qualities my actions for Christ will produce, what touchstone will tell me whether it is truly the passion of Christ which animates me. St. Paul had cautioned his Philippians: "In your minds you must be the same as Christ Jesus" (2:5). At the cross of Christ I know with certainty what mind this was.

One final conviction that I learn from the death of Christ: I live because he died: ". . .wherever we may be, we carry with us in our body the death of Jesus, so that the life of Jesus, too, may always be seen in our body" (2 Cor 4:10). In October, 1971, in Rome beatification ceremonies were held for Father Maximilian Kolbe, a Conventual Friar Minor from Poland, who had died in the concentration camp of Auschwitz. From the human point of view Father Maximilian's death could not have been more horrible. In retaliation for the successful escape of a few prisoners from the compound the Nazis had taken at random ten men from among the prisoners of the camp, condemning them to the appalling torture of death in a "hunger bunker." When it was learned that one of the ten prisoners was the father of a family, Father Maximilian stepped forward, volunteering to take this man's place, and the German commander unexpectedly accepted the offer. We can only imagine the sufferings of all ten of the prisoners, but especially of Father Maximilian, who, we know, was the last to die. Among those taking part in the beatification ceremonies at Rome was the man whom he had replaced. What are the thoughts of this man who must always be aware that he lives because this priest died for him? His whole life has been conditioned existentially, to its very roots, by what happened there in the concentration camp. He is radically affected and cannot live in just an ordinary way; his life has acquired tremendous value because of the price which has been paid for it, and he must live up to that value. Imagine that Father Kolbe's parents are still alive in a village somewhere in Poland and that this former prisoner visits them to tell them of their son's heroic self-immolation. Proud of their son, rejoicing in his magnificent generosity, the parents do not blame the living man. On the contrary, they accept him as their son, glad to acknowledge the special relationship which has been established between him and them through the death of their son.

This may help us to understand what St. Paul means when he reminds us that we always carry with us the death of Christ so that the life of Jesus may be seen in us. It is as though I too present myself before the Father of Jesus, reminding him of the death Christ willingly underwent for me, and he, seeing in me the life of his beloved Jesus, accepts me as his son. In a mysterious way I have become a continuation of the life of Jesus—this surely is one of the meanings of Christ's death. The conclusion is inescapable for anyone who wants to be fair: I cannot live henceforth just the way I like. I must live worthy of the price Christ has paid for me.

Remember, the ransom that was *paid to free you* from the useless way of life your ancestors handed down was not paid in anything corruptible, neither in silver nor gold, but in the

196

precious blood of a lamb without spot or stain, namely
Christ. . . (1 Pet 1:18-19).

St. Paul had no other message for his early Christians:

The reason Jesus died for all was so that living men should live
no longer for themselves, but for him who died and was raised
to life for them (2 Cor 5:15).

None of us lives as his own master and none of us dies as his
own master. While we live we are responsible to the Lord, and
when we die we die as his servants. Both in life and death we
are the Lord's. That is why Christ died and came to life again,
that he might be Lord of both the dead and the living (Rom
14:7-9, NAB).

Your body, you know, is the temple of the Holy Spirit, who is
in you since you received him from God. You are not your
own property; you have been bought and paid for. That is why
you should use your body for the glory of God (1 Cor
6:19-20).

Sixteen

THEIR EYES WERE OPENED

It is evening of the first Easter day, and two of the disciples of Jesus are on the road, making their way from Jerusalem to Emmaus (Lk 24:13-35). Unobtrusively, almost casually, Jesus joins them, travels along with them, and they do not recognize him—a symbol of the Church. Like the disciples, the Church is en route, on the way, journeying with Jesus whom we do not see: "You did not see him, yet you love him; and still without seeing him, you are already filled with a joy so glorious that it cannot be described, because you believe...." (1 Pet 1:8). Indeed, everything about the Church is a matter of faith. We do not see him, have never touched him, but we believe. At Emmaus the Lord, even though they do not recognize him, still changed their sadness into a joy which made their hearts burn within them and made of them apostles.

Because the story of Emmaus is very much our own story, we feel a close kinship with these men in their loneliness and despondency. We too know moments in which the whole faith seems merely a pious fantasy, a tremendous projection of our own making. Like the disciples, we seldom realize that it is exactly at such moments that the Lord is very close to us. The plea of Emmaus should always be ours: Stay with us, Lord. Sometimes it is dark around us and lonely in our hearts. Speak to us then, Lord, so that our hearts may really burn, so that something of your glory may come flooding into us and radiate from us. And then, after this petition we should indeed listen without being too busy. Prayer is above all a time of quiet and of listening so that God may have a chance to communicate, to speak to our hearts, to share that joy which the risen Lord has come to bring.

At Emmaus also we catch a glimpse of the role of the Christian apostle as consoler. It is appropriate to pray earnestly that the Lord will teach us how to bring solace to others, for this is something we owe to the risen Lord if we truly believe in him. To a world that does not know the joy of the resurrection we must be ministers of joy, encouraging and bringing comfort. Christian consolation has nothing superficial about it; a mere pat on the back or an apt compliment may have its place, of course, but that is never enough. We must seek to give genuine consolation, the solace that goes to the very depths of our existence, the strength that comes from faith. And because man's need for this is so great, we must not be shy or affected, but must have both the courage and the ability to speak out authentically. In this way we shall truly be disciples, men sent with the message of hope.

There is another prayer that features here, one wholly in keeping with the spirit of Easter. In the *Spiritual Exercises* St. Ignatius teaches us to ask for the grace "to be intensely glad and to rejoice in such great glory and joy of Christ Jesus our Lord." We must *ask* for this grace, ask continuously. Like the importunate widow who persisted in calling upon the judge until she was answered (Lk 18:1-5), we too must keep up our request. What we are asking for is a *grace*; that is, it cannot be provided by self. It has to be given. The joy we are seeking is not one which we ourselves can set in motion—music, companionship, distractions—nothing will provide it. God must give it, and in this way only shall we have the true grace to be intensely glad and to rejoice at the resurrection of our Lord. Furthermore we are asking for the grace to be *intensely glad*. This is not mere good humor; rather it is a deep-seated gladness and joy that pervade our whole being. One further point is that the object of this joy is not something in me, but in Jesus. We are asking for the grace of rejoicing in the great glory and joy *of our Lord Jesus Christ*. It is *his* joy which is to flood our being, to transform us. We are seeking to be glad because of the happiness he is experiencing. Compassion, the ability to suffer with a person who suffers, is truly a sign of love; but to rejoice with one who rejoices is a still greater sign of love, for somehow, it is easier to have compassion with the afflicted than to enter honestly and wholeheartedly into the joy of another, to be glad because *he* is glad. The prayer of Ignatius, then, boils down to a sincere and unselfish love for Christ: I ask that I may love him so much that *his* resurrection may fill my heart with utter gladness. If this prayer is heard, I shall have found a source of joy which is unassailable, for whatever happens, the Lord is always risen. Contingencies cannot suffocate this deep joy. Whether the day is fair or stormy, whether I am well or sick, whatever comes cannot alter the fact that the Lord is risen. If the resurrection of Jesus means enough to me, I shall always be happy: "All I want is to know Christ and the power of his resurrection. . . ." (Phil 3:10).

This matter of joy in the risen Lord has a great deal to do with faith, for a sad Christian is really not an authentic Christian. In this regard the words of Mother Teresa of Calcutta are impressive. She has devoted her life to the lowest forms of human misery; her days are wholly taken up with the sufferings and the sorrows of the most forsaken. And yet her words are unqualified: "Never let anything fill your heart with so much grief that you forget the joys of the risen Lord." These are the words of a woman of faith, a perfect example of the grace Ignatius means. Mother Teresa can work with the poor because she has Christ's own intense joy and gladness in her heart. It is this which makes her so radiant, so appealing. For this reason people flock to her, and she is able to console them truly, not just with money or medication—she has too little of these—but above all with the true consolation that comes from faith, the faith embodied in her own life.

On that first Easter day, however, there was no such joy in the hearts of the travelers to Emmaus: "they were talking together about all that had happened. Now as they talked this over, Jesus himself came up and walked by their side; but something prevented them from recognizing him." At first glance this seems puzzling, yet it is a constant feature of all the appearances of the risen Jesus that the disciples who had known him so well before his death do not recognize him after his resurrection. Mary Magdalen with all her intense love for Jesus mistakes him for the gardener. Later the fishing companions do not recognize the stranger at the shore until after the miraculous catch of fish—and this is not because of the morning haze. The gospels stress this feature of non-recognition to indicate that while Jesus is the same, he is completely changed. Many of us tend to underestimate the change brought about by the resurrection because we fail to grasp the cardinal point that the resurrection does not mean that Christ came back to this life. To think that he did is to miss the whole point of the mystery of the resurrection. Lazarus had died and had then returned to this life, but that was not a resurrection—it was merely a return to life. Christ did not come back to this life, however; he broke through death to a wholly new life. The key to an understanding of the true nature of Christ's resurrection is found in St. Paul's words to the Romans: "Death has no power over him any more" (6:9). The life of the risen Lord is one in which he is not going to die again. Lazarus, recalled from the tomb, would die a second time. That made a difference, and this difference is the vital point of the resurrection. If Christ lives a life over which death has no power, it means that he is the same Christ, but so intensely changed that even his best friends, his most faithful disciples, do not recognize him.

Resurrection means that in an actual continuity there occurs a tremendous discontinuity. "It is the same with the resurrection of the dead: the thing that is sown is perishable but what is raised is imperishable. . .It is sown a physical body, it is raised a spiritual body" (1 Cor 15:42,44). The truth of the resurrection is surely more than a subjective conviction. It is a reality, but of an order completely different from what we are accustomed to. It is the break-through of the eschatalogical reality into our familiar world, the beginning of a new creation. It is more real than that which we usually call reality; therefore, only the eye of faith can discern this super-real bodily presence of the Risen One. This faith-vision then enables us to recognize in the risen Jesus the Christ, our Lord and our God, a perception which is such a profound, personal experience that our life is totally changed: *metanoia.* We cannot avoid forming a mental image when we think of the risen Lord. It is simply part of our human condition that we cannot think without conceptualizing. This is all right as long as we know that our representation is decidedly inadequate. We cannot delineate the mystery of the resurrection; nevertheless we can be thoroughly inspired by it.

The two men on the road to Emmaus are sad. Asked why, they reply, "Because Christ has died." They are not unbelievers, men who had never heard of Christ or who, having heard, had rejected his message. On the contrary, they had really devoted their lives to Jesus of Nazareth. They had found new certainty in his presence, and they had loved this man with a true, human affection. Perhaps their affection had been too human. Perhaps there had been too little faith in it. For St. Paul it seemed enough that Christ should live in us through faith, when he admonished his Ephesians: "...that Christ may live in your hearts through faith...." (3:17). The disciples of Emmaus wanted signs to cling to, but the signs had been taken away. Now when they must live on faith alone, they discover how narrow is their faith which does not reach to the very end. They can enumerate readily enough the facts concerning Jesus, but significantly they tell over these facts exclusive of the resurrection. When Jesus acts as if he does not know what has happened, they begin their explanation:

'You must be the only person staying in Jerusalem who does not know the things that have been happening there these last few days.' 'What things?' he asked. 'All about Jesus of Nazareth' they answered, 'who proved he was a great prophet by the things he said and did in the sight of God and of the whole people; and how our chief priests and our leaders handed him over to be sentenced to death, and had him crucified. Our own hope had been that he would be the one to set Israel free. And this is not all: two whole days have gone by since it all happened....'

They can recite all too faithfully the account of the death of Christ, but they exclude the resurrection, and that makes all the difference. Faith without resurrection is gloomy, restless, despondent, unreal. On the other hand, faith including the resurrection is utterly different: it is a positive affirmation filled with peace, deep joy, and all the other fruits of the Spirit. Moreover, one who does not believe in the resurrection misunderstands not only the fact of this mystery but all that precedes it as well, for it is the last phase of the life of Christ which changes everything that has gone before. The great contribution of modern exegesis is that it has shown this relevancy of the resurrection for the whole of the New Testament, especially for the gospels. Here, if we delete the accounts of Christ's resurrection, we have nothing left. No life remains because we have taken away the life-blood with which they are infused. It is the resurrection which is the basis of our faith. Touch it, and the whole faith becomes gloomy, shaky, untrustworthy—and rightly so. St. Paul's words are unequivocal:

> If there is no resurrection of the dead, Christ himself cannot have been raised, and if Christ has not been raised then our preaching is useless and your believing is useless. . . .If our hope in Christ has been for this life only, we are the most unfortunate of all people (1 Cor 15:13-14,19).

The expression "basis of our faith" does not mean that the resurrection dispenses us in part from believing, let alone that the resurrection, as this basis, is exempt from faith. "Basis of our faith" means the ultimate of what we believe, that which makes our faith to be faith, the faith-fullness of our faith. It was faith in the resurrection which was lacking at Emmaus; that is why these men are so sad and why their faith is so depressed, finding nothing but disappointment in Christ. "Our hope had been...."—they had had it all figured out. They had thought that this rabbi of Nazareth would drive out the hated Romans and set them free, liberating them from the oppression of the humiliating occupation. This conquest of Jesus, the summation of all their desires, was one they themselves had devised. But it is not faith to have everything figured out. True faith is open-minded; it listens, it does not invent. It receives, but does not dictate. By their very lack of faith these disciples of Emmaus show that their real conversion is still to come.

There is another aspect of the basic weakness of their faith: they do not yet accept the mystery of the cross. Given their lack of faith in the resurrection, this makes sense, of course, since the cross and the resurrection are two sides of the same coin, of that single paschal mystery. So they had devised their plan of liberation, but had not taken into account the cross, having missed its value and its fruitfulness. Their faith had been tested by the cross, but they had failed the challenge, and having built their whole lives on their shallow, incomplete representation of Christ, they were left now with nothing but difficulties. Now their fantasy starts working, and they dream up all kinds of problems that might possibly happen—and even some impossible ones too! Thus they make each other sadder and sadder. Fantasy can be a tyrant which obsesses, stifling both faith and the spiritual life. Mark Twain, that shrewd old observer of life, once remarked: I am an old man now; I have known a lot of misery, but most of it has never happened! At Emmaus we see the disciples spreading their gloom, each adding to the desolation of the other, and thus rendering to each other a truly uncharitable disservice.

Then Christ comes. He will teach them the resurrection, but he can do so only by teaching them the theology of the cross. Actually, this is the most difficult chapter in all of theology, for some an obstacle they cannot surmount, for others sheer madness (cf. 1 Cor 1:23-24). Christ began his lesson straightway: "Was it not ordained that the Christ should suffer and so enter into his glory?" Here we have once again that mysterious connection between suffering and glory which Christ had tried to teach many times, but always he had failed; his disciples simply had not understood. There are in the gospel at least three major prophecies of the passion:

> From that time Jesus began to make it clear to his disciples that he was destined to go to Jerusalem and suffer grievously at the hands of the elders and chief priests and scribes, to be put to death and to be raised up on the third day. Then, taking him aside, Peter started to remonstrate with him. 'Heaven preserve you, Lord,' he said, 'this must not happen to you' (Mt 16:21-22).

Thus, Christ's first prophecy of the passion was a failure. He tried again:

> At a time when everyone was full of admiration for all he did, he said to his disciples, 'For your part, you must have these words constantly in your mind: The Son of Man is going to be handed over into the power of men.' But they did not understand him when he said this; it was hidden from them so that they should not see the meaning of it. . . (Lk 9:43-45).

He was no more successful here, so he tried a third time, adding more specific details:

207

> Then taking the Twelve aside he said to them, 'Now we are going up to Jerusalem, and everything that is written by the prophets about the Son of Man is to come true. For he will be handed over to the pagans and will be mocked, maltreated and spat on, and when they have scourged him they will put him to death; and on the third day he will rise again.' But they could make nothing of this; what he said was quite obscure to them, they had no idea what it meant (Lk 18:31-34).

The disciples had missed all these lessons on the meaning of the passion, but the matter was too valuable to be lost, so once again at Emmaus Christ, the rabbi, took· up in a private lesson this subject which was proving so difficult: "Then, starting with Moses and going through all the prophets, he explained to them the passages throughout the scriptures that were about himself."

The exegesis of the scriptures continued during the journey to Emmaus, but the lesson was not to end there on the road. The climax that would make clear the whole was still to come in the meal that followed their urgent invitation. At this supper table the guest becomes the host and performs those tasks which are proper to the host: he breaks the bread and speaks the blessing. Now comes that moment of tremendous intimacy between the disciples and the Lord; their eyes are opened and they recognize him in the breaking of the bread. In every Eucharist the theology of the cross is celebrated in both the death-aspect and the resurrection-aspect of the paschal mystery. Such a celebration can prove a powerfully enlightening experience for the worshiper.

There is a final reflection to be made on the incident at Emmaus. In the very moment of their glad recognition of the risen Christ, the men feel impelled to set out immediately for Jerusalem to share the good news with the others. Once a person has met the risen Lord, he is transformed into an apostle who must spread abroad the message he has received. In a way, these poor disciples are rather amusing. A few minutes earlier they had been pressing Jesus to remain because it was so late. Now, however, it is not too late for them to retrace immediately the seven long miles to Jerusalem because they have good news to share. They find the apostles where they had left them, but these too were changed men, and they have their own story to tell. "Yes, it is true," they said, "the Lord has risen and has appeared to Simon." The men from Emmaus then shared with the disciples of Jerusalem "what had happened on the road and how they had recognized him at the breaking of the bread."

The episode which began with two sad men on the road ends with an apostolic community happily rejoicing. It is the risen Lord who has made the difference. He has driven out the despondency and the bitterness, transforming them into joy and fruitfulness. When we really love him and believe in his resurrection, we cannot hold on to grief and resentment, but we must surrender these feelings to him as being out of place. This may well be a difficult capitulation because grief, especially when caused by injustice, tends to become ingrained. Yet how can we be messengers of the Good News if we ourselves are bad news! Indeed, we owe him our disappointments. If we cannot rid ourselves of them, then let us expose them to the radiant power of the risen Lord so that he may heal our wounds and create the community that is held together through joyous faith in the resurrection. This kind of witnessing made the early Church at once apostolic and appealing. It is still the only way to render apostolate convincing.

Seventeen

THE OPENED DOOR

"I have opened in front of you a door that nobody will be able to close" (Rev 3:8). Every biblical image, at once simple and profound, is an invitation to reach to the level of transcendence, to see encased in figure a truth of such depth that it helps us to perceive readily a new dimension of reality. This text from Revelations is an example of one such image, for immediately it brings us face to face with a multiplicity of meanings, all of which converge on the open door as a symbol of faith, an invitation to go out from the more confining limits of our every-day surroundings and to experience the liberating, often exhilirating effect of a journey to new lands, to a new understanding of what is meant by a life of faith. "*I have opened a door*"—faith is always a gift, and we have only to read the gospels to see how deeply concerned Christ was that we might accept this gift, that we might be a believing people. And it is an *open door*, one that always represents a call to further discovery. The connection between a journeying forth—an exodus—and faith is a constant theme of scriptures.

Why should the sheikh of nomads, Abram, emigrate? Not for his children surely because at the time of his exodus he did not have any, nor could he realistically have expected to have any in the future. Yet he begins what must have seemed a foolish adventure, hoping that his emigration will benefit his posterity. Why should Moses go to Pharaoh, asking that he free the people of Israel from the concentration camp where they were working for him? There seemed not the slightest chance that Pharaoh would consent; on the contrary, it was dangerous to come with a request like that. Yet Moses does venture all—and he wins. It was the same with Joshua and the judges, with David and the kings, with all the prophets—time and again they show this same "vision"; in spite of all powers and threats, they hazard everything for their people and they succeed. And in the long history of such events there grows an experiential knowledge in Israel, the unshakable conviction that Yahweh is not only a promising, a demanding God; he is also reliable. This reliability of Yahweh will form the backbone of Israel's faith, and it will enable the people to hope against hope and to overcome.

Faith is always an invitation to cross borders, to take advantage of the opening in a horizon become too constricting. It is the vista of a new perspective opening to me when I feel oppressed, a call to experience an exodus when I feel trapped. How many are the borders which faith opens to me! There is, first of all, the call of faith to cross the narrow borders of my own concepts of God. In place of the limited, myopic view I have of God, faith teaches me of his vastness, his transcendence. I can never fully grasp him, for no notion does justice to his true greatness. It is faith which helps me to understand that to know God means constantly to be on the move: "Here we have no lasting city" (Heb 13:14, NAB). The search for God, therefore, is a perpetual going forth, a continual crossing over into a new, more profound understanding of who God is and what he is like.

Faith also opens for me a universe that may have become closed. It helps me to understand that the world is not mere confinement, that human experience is more than a vortex into which I have been cast. On the contrary, faith opens a new perspective and meaning to life and to all that exists. It is this meaningfulness which releases oppression, dethrones exacting and restraining idols, saves from degrading substitutes.

Nor is this all, for faith does not halt at the confines of life. It means also a crossing over the border of death itself. Faith shows us not only that God wants us to live, but that he is concerned with more than a lifetime in this world. The latter would be far too little to satisfy God's tremendous yearning for my being. God wants me to live forever, and it is faith which enables me to see that in his mighty hand I am held safe not only in life, but even beyond its borders in death itself. We believe in a God of the living. It is faith which leads me to understand how his measure is endless, how a lifetime cannot exhaust it.

Faith also helps me to achieve that understanding of my fellowmen which makes all human association possible, and even the generation gap can be overcome by its light. The very last verse of the Old Testament had promised such an outcome: "The Prophet Elijah shall turn the hearts of fathers towards their children and the hearts of children towards their fathers" (Mal 3:24). Zechariah had heard the angel of God apply this prophecy to John the Baptist: "With the spirit and power of Elijah, he will go before him to turn the hearts of fathers towards their children and the disobedient back to the wisdom that the virtuous have, preparing for the Lord a people fit for him" (Lk 1:17). It is faith which helps us to understand each other and to cross the frontiers that separate generations.

It is not only my relations with others which faith assists, however; I am helped by its means to escape being locked in the guilt of my past, for faith offers the priceless gift of reconciliation: "...for anyone who is in Christ, there is a new creation; the old creation has gone, and the new one is here. It is all God's work. It was God who reconciled us to himself through Christ" (2 Cor 5:17-18). By opening for me a way out of my guilt and into this new creation, faith removes that most severe of human sufferings—the pain of knowing that I have done wrong— and turns it into a more profound experience of God's faithfulness.

Possibly the most deeply personal invitation that faith gives me is the call to cross the borders within myself. It brings home to me the tremendous truth that I can change, that *metanoia* as a deep reorientation of my whole outlook is possible, that I can truly become different. We are not fixed immovably in that way in which we were born, but the strength of God, the strength of faith, can bring about a true salvation, a liberation. Faith means that I know myself accepted by God *as I am*, and when I am convinced of this, then I can accept myself as I am. In fact, genuine self-acceptance is an act of faith. It may be feared that the kind of faith which leads to self-acceptance will put an end to all striving, to all desire for change, and that under its effect all effort will grind to a halt. Nothing could be more untrue. To accept oneself as one is does not mean to be resigned to the status quo and leave it at that. On the contrary, the more fully we accept ourselves, the more successfully we can change ourselves. Love is a far better stimulus than threat or pressure. St. Thérèse of Lisieux used to say that she was the type of woman who advances more rapidly when she is drawn by love than when she is driven by fear. She was keen enough to know that we are all that type of person. It is possible to become a saint while still being prone to sensuality and envy, to pettiness and insincerity, but the first move will always be to recognize that one is that way. When parents of a stuttering child are annoyed by this defect, they may tend to rebuke the child, insisting that he repeat the phrases over which he has stumbled. Obviously, a more effective way to help the child would be not to make impatient comments about the defect. But it is equally obvious that silence in itself will be of no help unless it is the fruit of an inner acceptance of the child with his defect. As long as the parents resent the inadequacy of the child, they will subconsciously exert pressure on him, and by so doing they aggravate the situation and prevent its cure. Each of us is in a similar situation, and when we resent or ignore our defects, we put pressure on ourselves, a pressure which prevents healing or improvement. In this matter of self-improvement the belief that God accepts me as I am is a tremendous help to become better.

Faith means to cross borders, but at the exact point where the frontier can be penetrated. Faith is not an escape from reality, a flight into Utopia, a strange, unrealistic refuge from life. There is only one point at which this crossing can be made, and this is in imitation of Christ. It is only along the narrow path on which Christ leads that we can really pierce the frontier, the same road on which he himself journeyed when through his death he started a new life, one in which anguish and suffering and death have no longer a place: "Now I am making the whole of creation new" (Rev 21:5). It is precisely at this point that faith achieves the perspective of hope.

Hope and faith are ineradicably joined. Hope is not just an accidental accretion to faith; it is an absolutely indispensable consequence of truly believing, just as it is a necessary condition for living a life of faith. I can well propose as a test for my faith the question: Am I useful as a witness to hope? Nor is hope a test of my faith only; it is also a test of my love: "...[love] is always ready...to hope" (1 Cor 13:7). By its very nature hope proves the caliber of our faith and of our love. Pessimism is never a fruit of the Spirit, we know, but there may be a danger that we confuse its opposite and see optimism as identical with hope. This is untrue, for hope has a much deeper foundation than mere optimism. The latter tries always to emphasize the positive aspects of life and to de-emphasize the negative aspects of reality. Helpful as such an attitude may be, it lacks the depth which the divine virtue of hope has. Hope is based in God's love as embodied in Jesus Christ's life, death, and resurrection. "The mystery is Christ among you, your hope of glory" (Col 1:27). Hope, therefore, is a kind of optimism which the world can never provide. St. Paul readily grasped the connection between hope and faith. Writing to his Ephesians (2:12) he mentions in one breath people "without hope and without God," and to the believers in Thessalonika he speaks about "the other people who have no hope" (1 Thess 4:13).

Hope means to believe in an absolute love, i.e., in a God who is love, which means a love having neither conditions nor limitations. When hope is lacking, no matter how profound or how modern we may be when we speak of faith, we can be sure that faith is lacking as well, for in reality, hope is a concretization of faith. It is hope which continually renews and inspires our faith. At the same time, hope is the fruit of our faith: "May the God of hope bring you such joy and peace in your faith that the power of the Holy Spirit will remove all bounds to hope" (Rom 15:13). Hope prevents us from settling down, taking things for granted. It implies that we aim high and are never satisfied with what has been reached so far. Unlike optimism, hope perceives sharply the failures in the present situation. When we really hope, we cannot compromise with the establishment, but on the contrary, we must work for a better world. And yet, if it is truly hope that is inspiring us, we shall do this without bitterness or fanaticism. Hope enables us to work for peace in a peaceful way: ". . .always have your answer ready for people who ask you the reason for the hope that you all have. But give it with courtesy and respect and with a clear conscience" (1 Pet 3:15).

In the second half of Romans 8 we find Paul's hymn of hope, just as in the thirteenth chapter of 1 Corinthians we read his hymn of love. The hymn concludes with a ringing affirmation of Christian hope:

> For I am certain of this: neither death nor life, no angel, no prince, nothing that exists, nothing still to come, not any power, or height or depth, nor any created thing, can ever come between us and the love of God made visible in Christ Jesus our Lord (Rom 8:38-39).

We are not surprised to find that this paean on hope was a favorite passage of Teilhard de Chardin. It is a song of cosmic joy, thereby creating an atmosphere in which God can be found everywhere: "I think that what we suffer in this life can never be compared to the glory, as yet unrevealed, which is waiting for us" (Rom 8:18). This may sound like an over-statement. We think of all the injustices and tortures in the world today about which Amnesty International reports, of the hatred between Jews and

Arabs, of the terrible feelings of depression some people have to undergo, or a realization of guilt which can be such a tremendously corrosive burden. We think of our own anxieties and infidelities, of our restlessness and shallowness. St. Paul does not want to gloss over any of these, but he knows that true faith integrates even the most negative human experiences, that it enables us to face the suffering that is going on and to present it to our God, and then in the name of God to fight this evil. In this way our very suffering can become a new link in our relations with God. When we keep anything apart from our relations with God, it will tend to become an entity in itself, causing cleavage in our lives. But when we manage to integrate everything into our relations with God, then everything becomes a positive means of strengthening the tie which binds us to God and of deepening the covenant.

"It is through hope that we are saved" (Rom 8:24). St. Paul then gives a little phenomenology of hope. We should not have to be hoping for something if it were in sight; i.e., hope is not yet vision. This is the constant lesson of the New Testament: "Happy are those who have not seen and yet believe" (Jn 20:29). "You did not see him, yet you love him..." (1 Pet 1:8). "Only faith can guarantee the blessings that we hope for, or prove the existence of the realities that at present remain unseen" (Heb 11:1). We are brought once more to the truth: the foundation of hope is faith. We attempt to improve the world and to become ourselves better people not because we perceive in ourselves the strength to accomplish this, but because we believe that everything is possible with God and that God's power is at its best in our weakness (2 Cor 12:9).

The second characteristic of hope which Paul mentions is perseverance and steadfastness. "It is something we must wait for with patience" (v. 25). Our hope should not be a reed swaying with the breeze; rather it should be anchored in the solid rock, the deepest Ground of all that exists. This implies that hope excludes restlessness, all fidgetiness. Hope is the mother of patience, without which no hope can subsist. When hope is lacking, there is need for agitation and sensation, whose symptoms are a stream of many words with little content, a curiosity, a certain interior and exterior unquiet. Real hope makes us intent on that for which we hope, and by so doing it creates a certain recollectedness. However, the steadfastness of hope is a redeemed steadfastness. It is not merely a stubborn obstinacy based on our own inflexibility.

The third characteristic of hope is that it expresses itself in prayer: "For when we cannot choose words in order to pray properly, the Spirit himself expresses our plea in a way that could never be put into words" (v. 26). Prayer is like the breathing of hope. It is the reaching out for our goal, and the Spirit himself leads us in that prayer.

In the last part of his hymn on hope Paul concretizes the content of hope in the person of Jesus Christ. All our hope is founded in him. Everything happening in our lives is meant to transform us into more faithful images of Jesus Christ. That is what gives meaning to our lives. We are convinced that everything can help to bring us closer to that imitation and likeness of Christ, and in Jesus we are sure that God's love is with us always. "Since God did not spare his own Son, but gave him up to benefit us all, we may be certain, after such a gift, that he will not refuse anything he can give" (v. 32). We discover that nothing can ever come between us and the love of God made visible in

Christ Jesus our Lord. Not troubles, nor worries, nor persecutions, nor lack of food and clothes, nor threats, nor attacks, nor death, nor life, nor anything whatever can come between us and the love of God made visible in Christ Jesus. From 2 Cor 11:23-33, we know that Paul understands what he is talking about. There he is enumerating the hardships he has endured for the sake of his apostolate. Paul himself is a proof that everything can cooperate for our good when we really try to love God. He was not embittered by disappointments, hardships, sufferings. On the contrary, these made him all the more the ecstatic and generous apostle who lived on hope and could convey that hope to many others. May we learn from him that our hope too can grow by our giving it to others.

THE WEALTH OF TOGETHERNESS

Yahweh, our Lord,
how great your name throughout the earth!
. . .

I look up at your heavens, made by your fingers,
at the moon and stars you set in place—
ah, what is man that you should spare a thought for him,
the son of man that you should care for him?

Yet you have made him little less than a god,
you have crowned him with glory and splendoi,
made him lord over the work of your hands,
set all things under his feet,

sheep and oxen, all these,
yes, wild animals too,
birds in the air, fish in the sea
traveling the paths of the ocean.

Yahweh, our Lord
how great your name throughout the earth! (from Ps 8).

We find here the praises of God sung because of the
greatness and dignity he has given to man, a greatness
established by man's power over nature. In our days we
have far more power over nature than the psalmist could
ever have dreamed. We have put men on the moon, have

transplanted human hearts, have created rapid, world-wide communication systems, have unlocked nuclear energy, have compounded the most intricate medicines and therapies, have built immensely complex computers. Yet if we are called upon to elaborate the greatness of man, it is to his inter-personal relations that we turn, the inter-relatedness of men, the enduring link of man to man, our human solidarity. These are the values that appeal today. Recently a large Dutch newspaper ran a recruiting advertisement for student-nurses, with the headlines: "Nurse, can you apply a dressing as well as establish a relationship? We challenge you!" This advertisement zeroes in on what young people today consider of value. That we are involved in one another means far more than all our advanced technology and expertise. Mankind forms a huge net, whose nodal points are neither the gadgets of technology nor the ideas of the philosophers, but rather people. One reason for the success of Teilhard de Chardin is precisely his emphasis on the unity of mankind. Following his line of reasoning, we can say: I come from a family where I became who I am. My father and mother, my brothers and sisters shaped me to what I am. The great majority of my opinions, of my likes and dislikes, of my values and appreciations have been stamped by that family. This familial touch reaches deep into my subconscious: my prejudices, my a priori judgments, my behavior, my taste, my logic are molded by the family I come from. No man is self-made.

The next step is to realize that my family was part of a specific culture. In my case, this is Holland, a part of the Western hemisphere. If I had been the son of a Chinese Zen-master or of an Egyptian fellah, I would have been a different person because my family, itself shaped by another culture, would have been different.

We can go further still. I am part of mankind, and therefore, I carry within myself the experiences of joys and anguishes which are not my own personal ones, but which have grown in me from hundreds of thousands of years of human history. The "phenomenon of man" is the fruit of billions of years of evolution, of which we have only a tiny fragment of knowledge. Moreover, that evolution is still going on, drawing mankind toward an ever greater unity until it will reach its completion in point Omega, when Christ will be the pleroma, the "everything-in-one," the "all-in-all," the fullness of creation.

Each man is linked with his fellowmen. Since no one is truly a separate individual, it is only in union with others that our lives become meaningful. That is why today the trend in our lives places growing emphasis on the team. Science provides a good example of this: in the first decades of this century, great discoveries were still the work of gifted individuals such as Thomson, Planck, Bohr, Einstein. After World War II, however, there was a shift. Articles now were written not by one man, but by a whole group of authors, sometimes as many as fifteen, whose names were all listed at the head of the publication. Around 1960 this movement became still more marked when the names of the individual scientists were often dropped and only the team was mentioned. This enlargement is typical of modern science. Or think of the first trip to the moon, during which 40,000 people, strategically placed across the world, were available at any moment for information or assistance. When Armstrong set his foot on the moon, he rightly voiced thanks to the numerous persons behind the scenes who had made possible this "little giant step." A single heart-transplantation may involve from a dozen to a score of surgeons. In psychology we have group-dynamics; in psychiatry, group-sessions. In the apostolate today we speak of pastoral teams, and in religious life much more than in the past the emphasis is on authentic living-community. Even the saint of the future, it was recently said, would be more a team of God-filled people than a single individual.

Examples such as these stress the idea that in our days a person is like a juncture of relations. In the sixth century Boethius gave his famous definition of "person," which was later adopted by St. Thomas Aquinas and for centuries prevailed in Western thought: "A person is an individual substance of a rational nature." There is no mention of relations to others in this definition. To correct this, Martin Buber in our day says, "In the beginning there is the relation." During the nineteenth and early twentieth centuries religious built enormous monasteries and convents which at one time were very impressive. What impresses nowadays, however, is not a large building nor even a large number of religious, but a group that forms a true community. I once visited a Trappist abbey where I was told that the abbot who had built it around 1910 had wanted it to be the largest abbey in the Order. Whether he achieved his ideal or not I do not know, but he certainly set up a huge monastery! I am sure that such an ideal would have no appeal for our generation. What counts for us is that the monks in that building live authentic relations of brotherly love. It is not the physical size of the building nor the number of religious that refer us to God, but the quality of their relations of friendship, love, and unity.

224

In the ceremony of the vows we used to stress the obligations and responsibilities which the newly professed religious took upon himself. Today we emphasize also the duties which the community accepts in receiving this new member. Sharing with others is an essential aspect of the vows. Each religious community should be an epiphany of what the Church really means: that we are all children of one Father and that we realize among ourselves that unity for which Jesus prayed in his priestly prayer and which he declared necessary if he was truly to be recognized for what he is:

> Father, may they be one in us,
> as you are in me and I am in you,
> so that the world may believe it was you who sent me. . .
> With me in them and you in me,
> may they be so completely one
> that the world will realize that it was you who sent
> me (Jn 17:21,23).

What Irenaeus said centuries ago is still true: "The glory of God is the living man." (*Gloria Dei vivens homo.*) But today we immediately add the qualification that a man who lives by himself is not fully living. We like the parable of the Last Judgment (Mt 25:31-46) and we often quote it: if you never share your food with a hungry man, etc., you have not come to fulfillment as a human being; you are a true Christian only in sharing with others. And we love Pope John for saying, "As long as there is one man behind bars, I myself am not free." We realize that it is impossible first to become a person and then to relate to others, that it is only in relation with others that one can become a person. In the dense phrase of Buber: "Man

225

becomes 'I' through 'you'." (*Der Mensch wird am Du zum Ich.*) In his beautiful story of the encounter of the little prince with the fox Antoine de Saint-Exupéry made the same point in a more elaborate way.[1] What I do, what I am concerns other people as well as myself. To the degree that this is not so, I am not yet fully myself and my humanity has not yet reached full stature. We really need each other to be ourselves. It is obvious that the weak people need the strong ones, and it is Christian that the strong ones need the weak. "We who are strong have a duty to put up with the qualms of the weak without thinking of ourselves. Each of us should think of his neighbors...Christ did not think of himself" (Rom 15:1-3). The delicacy with which we communicate this sense of solidarity is in itself a manifestation of our human need for one another. Ladislaus Boros has observed:

> Perhaps we shall not be able to cure illness or even relieve pain by our visit. We can do one thing at least: show the sick, most probably without saying so, merely by our presence, that they are a grace for us, that the world would be unthinkable and unendurable without the support of those who suffer.[2]

Indeed, the weak can bring out the best in the strong, and thus both can in their mutual dependence grow as human persons. To write off the weak would mean the end of Christian community. Having been abbot for almost the whole of his life, St. Bernard knew well how difficult community life could be. Yet with tongue in cheek he could preach in a homily to his monks:

> If in an abbey at a certain moment there happens to be no monk who is a burden and a cross to his fellow-monks,

something very precious and even essential would be lacking in that monastery. And so the abbot would have to go on a journey to visit a neighboring abbey in order to borrow a monk like that for the time being.

Both the wisdom and the sense of humor of the saint are refreshing!

In religious life there may arise a situation which, while not universal, occurs frequently enough to be mentioned here. It can happen that some in a religious community who neglect the spiritual life (in the sense of celebrating the Eucharist, communal and personal prayer, meditation especially on holy scripture, serious and inspiring spiritual reading, etc.) experience difficulties with the community in which they live. At times they tend to project their own spiritual sloth on their community, complaining about a lack of mutual support and inspiration. Probably in many cases the explanation of the phenomenon is that these people lack the ability to accept the weaknesses of others and look more for what the community can do for them than for what they can do for the group. Therefore, they are incapable of forming a real community. But such a spirit runs directly counter to the constant theme of sacred scriptures, for both the Old and New Testament are replete with instances which show that the purpose of the covenant is not only to unite man with God but also to unite man with his fellow man. Let Ecclesiastes speak for the Old Testament: "Woe to the man by himself" (Qo 4:10), and for the New Testament let us point to the significant fact that in the Our Father there is no "I" but only "we."

From the very first pages of Genesis Yahweh appears as the One who unifies the chaos into the universe and the individualistic nomads in an Egyptian concentration camp into a people, his chosen people at that. And the concluding pages of the gospel with the coming of the Holy Spirit bring full circle this theme of human solidarity in and through God.

> The Spirit came to the community, not to individuals. Though the Risen One appeared to individuals before he sent his Spirit, ever since this moment, individuals receive the Spirit and the presence of the Risen One only through the community. The Spirit animates a Body, not monads. Each new cell or dead cell comes to life through the touch of other members of the Body of Christ who are animated by the Spirit. Even the audacious singularity of Paul, the Apostle, had to await the ministrations of Ananias before he could be baptized and filled with the Holy Spirit. The loner who claims he is being led by the Spirit is a liar.[3]

Eighteen B

THE POVERTY OF UNIQUENESS

Community does not mean merely the juxtaposition of similar individuals, a collectivity of people very much alike. In fact, community can truly exist only when each person is different. There is a fundamental opposition between unity and uniformity; unity differentiates, thereby creating pluriformity, while uniformity, when it is imposed on a community, stifles life. We have seen many examples of this. When the liturgy was obligatory in Latin throughout the world, the price paid for this uniformity was that most people did not understand what was being said or sung. In religious life the renewal has often unmasked uniformity as a facade for a unity that turned out to be hardly existent. But the renewal in itself has not removed all dangers. When in a contemporary small community people are too compatible, the deeper union is threatened and there arises serious danger of a new type of superficial uniformity.

Community presupposes the irreplaceable uniqueness of each of its members. A football team of eleven quarterbacks will never make it. That is why for the building of community it is more important to stress that each person should be his own true self than to emphasize that a team must be formed. When we really help each person to become himself authentically, we indirectly stimulate community life. But if we begin by stressing community-living, we may well end with a kind of false security, a web of shallow coziness and infantile relations. Contact with others presupposes that one has contact with himself. In the Blessed Trinity the difference between the three Persons as Persons is so great that a greater difference cannot be conceived, yet their unity is so intense that a more intense unity cannot exist.

Each member of a community has a unique, very personal mission. No one can guarantee the vocation of another, nor insure his authenticity. No one can even probe the depth of the mystery of another human being. A person is very much like one of those magnificent and mysterious creatures whose home is in the depths of the sea. Bring one of them to the surface for close inspection, however, and it will explode before your eyes. This inexorable mystery of the human person makes him what he is—great and at the same time lonely. There is a certain amount of deep, inescapable loneliness if one wants to be authentic and tries to build true community.

Henri Nouwen has offered an analysis of this aspect of the human condition, pointing out that the Christian way of life, far from repudiating this sense of loneliness, sees it instead as something to be cherished. Rather than attempting to avoid a painful confrontation with loneliness by turning to false gods promising immediate satsifaction, we can see in this sense of isolation an invitation to transcend our human limitations, to expand our vision of what we truly are. It may well be that the recognition of our essential loneliness will help us to understand that inner emptiness which is waiting to be filled and which can be filled only by a truly Christian response. Viewed in this sense, our emptiness becomes not a destructive force but an invitation to hope. To live with loneliness, however, requires long patience; if we turn impulsively to what may give immediate relief, inevitably we shall cover up the real problem, and what had begun full of promise ends in tragic failure. Father Nouwen concludes:

> We ignore what we already know. . .that no love or friendship, no intimate embrace or tender kiss, no community, commune or collective, no man or woman, will ever be able to satisfy our desire. . . .This truth is so disconcerting and painful that we are more prone to play games with our fantasies than to face the truth of our existence. Thus we keep hoping that one day we will find the man who really understands our experiences, the woman who will bring peace to our restless life, the job where we can fulfill our potentials, the book which will explain everything, and the place where we can feel at home. Such false hope leads us to make exhausting demands and prepares us for bitterness and dangerous hostility when we start discovering that nobody, and nothing, can live up to our absolutistic expectations. Many marriages are ruined because neither partner was able to fulfill the often hidden hope that the other would take his or her loneliness away. And many celibates live with the naive dream that in the intimacy of marriage their loneliness will be taken away. When the minister lives with these false expectations and illusions he prevents himself from claiming his own loneliness as a source of human understanding, and is unable to offer any real service to the many who do not understand their own suffering.[1]

The violin and the guitar with their various, distinct strings, can produce beautiful music and inspiration, but concord and harmony can result only when this distinction of tone is preserved. And in the best marriages there is always the pain of not being able to identify as completely with the partner as one could wish: there remains always an inaccessible resource of mystery in the other, and the

231

consequent anguish of not being able to share everything completely.

A medieval Dutch *ballade* develops this theme poetically: a prince and princess, deeply in love, are unable to reach one another because a wide body of water separates them. Desirous of being united with his beloved, the young prince attempts to swim across, but when he has almost attained the shore, he is drowned by a wicked witch. The song symbolizes aptly how love is destroyed when we attempt to come too close, to penetrate the zone of mystery that necessarily surrounds the other.

This truth has two dimensions: first, if I want to build community, I must have the courage to be myself. Secondly, in order to make true brotherhood possible, I must grant the other person the right to be himself.

1. The courage to be myself constitutes the first condition.

I must truly be myself, different from everybody else, not yielding to the pressure to conform, not even giving in to the temptation constantly to be comparing myself with others. In an affluent society there is a trend to keep up with the Joneses, to allow ourselves to become brainwashed by advertising techniques. I consider this a serious threat leading inevitably to decadence and inauthenticity. This same phenomenon of conforming is found also in faith, in the Church, in religious life. Here too we notice a tendency to be "in" and "with it," and there is the disturbing impression that the impact of this tendency is becoming considerable. About four years ago I received a letter from a sister who had been present at an assembly of her Congregation in which 110 members had participated. She wrote:

The Poverty of Uniqueness

I heard so many ideas about prayer, especially from my own age-group. All this about body-person, no need for definite time, prayer as merely active living or personal relationships, experience of nature or music, etc., etc. So *many* are *convinced* and really believe a whole new reality of prayer concept is a must for Christian survival. If that is what they believe, I want to be open to their ideas. But I just cannot buy it and find myself drawn to quiet times and places, set apart from my work. Yet it is lonely to think differently, and since I am not yet thirty, maybe I should be more "with it." Much is good, but I often wonder if it is really that backward to be present in a time set aside to God and his written legacy? Or to be united with the Church and the great saints in the psalms? I often fear that maybe I'm not on the right track, or that my track is not headed for any future of religious life. Yet, I get so sick of this "shared stuff" and wonder if a craving for constant talk and sharing isn't a substitute/compensation for the hard-core task of letting Christ become the still point in the turning world of activity. I wonder where it will all lead. All I know is that I want to love, pray and serve, and wish that even in the hectic existence of American life this desire would become uncomplicated and direct.

When I reread this letter, what strikes me most is the realization of how much has changed in the trends within religious life in less than five years. Yet I am printing this passage (with the explicit permission of the sister who wrote it) because it states so clearly how the real problem is not prayer, but what others say. Do I have the courage to follow my conscience when others talk differently? Do I have the courage to be myself? Or shall I keep up with the Joneses?

Johann Metz has used the phrase "poverty of uniqueness" to express this sense of isolation which arises when the individual man responds to his own deeply personal mission that constitutes him alone among his fellow men. It was this aspect of inner poverty in Jesus which Satan attacked, trying to lure him through his inducements to be like other men—to feed on bread, to seek wealth or worldly prestige. And it is the same temptation each one of us must face: to turn aside from the poverty of our own uniqueness and to be like everyone else—to conform, to see in the will of the crowd the will of God. Such conformity can lead only to mediocrity—a mediocrity, Father Metz adds, which

> . . .is veiled and protected by the legalities, conventions and flattery of a society which craves endorsement for every activity, yet retreats into public anonymity. Indeed with such anonymity it will risk everything—and nothing—except a genuine, open, personal commitment. Yet without paying the price of poverty implied in such commitments, no one will fulfill his mission as a human being.

and he concludes: "Only this poverty of uniqueness enables us to find true selfhood."[2] We might add: "and true community as well." In authentic brotherhood there is inevitably a certain amount of loneliness, but fear of that loneliness is eliminated by the authenticity of the community. We may even find in this a good criterion with which to distinguish immature from genuine friendships and relationships.

2. Respect for the uniqueness which renders the other person different is the second dimension of genuine community.

A friendship can exist only by letting the other person *be other*, and by virtue of the mystery which the other person will always remain. The more intimately two people love, the more they confirm their being different. To know a person well on this level means to acknowledge and to accept the fact that there is always more to be known; one never exhausts the potential of the beloved. In her beautiful novel about a truly magnificent marriage Anne Philipe expresses this in the words of the wife, "We know one another so well that each of us can finish the sentence which the other begins, and yet the least of his gestures has more mystery in it than the smile of the Mona Lisa."[3] Only a deep respect for the continuance of this mystery can create the atmosphere in which marriage or friendship or community can grow and blossom. Respect is the heart of love, just as lack of respect is its end. Without respect there can be at best only a condescending charity which does more harm than good. What is worse, without true respect love can easily deteriorate into possessiveness or manipulation, essentially a negation of love. The more intense the love, the deeper the pain of the loneliness involved, for not only do I have to bear the pain of knowing that I shall never be able to penetrate completely the one I love so dearly, but I am also condemned to fall short in letting the other person enter into my own being. I thus experience the pain of knowing that I am causing the one I love most to suffer. This mystery of human relationships was cast by Chekhov into the paradox: "If you are afraid of loneliness, do not marry!"

It is obvious that if marriage has this pain of loneliness, religious celibacy has even greater solitude. And yet, if a religious does not accept this loneliness for himself and does not grant it to others, he can never build community. The inability to cope with this sense of aloneness almost always has a malignant effect both on the person himself and on his relations with others, for often it leads him to seek an escape in substitutes alien to his way of life. On the other hand, the ability to be alone is an irreplaceable condition for the capacity to build community, yes, even for the capacity to love.

Eighteen C

RESTLESS IS OUR HEART

The foregoing pages have emphasized two complementary features: community is a condition for personality, and personality is a condition for community. Albert Camus, quoting Victor Hugo, summarizes these points in two words: *solidaire et solitaire* (united and alone). Each one, divorced from the other, constitutes a danger. Solitude without community can be an escape into isolation, self-complacency, harshness, even despair. On the other hand, community without solitude can be an abuse of other persons in order to escape self.

The paradox of togetherness and loneliness makes sense only when we transcend both. The individual does not exist for the community, nor does the community exist for the individual, but both community and individual serve a higher purpose. Just as a man who forgets his preoccupation with being a person is most near to being one, so a community which overcomes its concern about itself is probably the best community (cf. Lk 17:33: "Anyone who tries to preserve his life will lose it; and anyone who loses it will keep it safe"). A sincere focusing on Jesus Christ and his gospel-message, an authentic apostolic endeavor, an attempt to genuine prayerfulness, a radical living of the evangelical vows can help both the individual and the community to rise above themselves.

Father James Connor, provincial of the Jesuits in Maryland, has commented upon the dangers encountered when this apostolic challenge is lacking:

...undue and disproportionate stress is put upon community as the locus of *intimate friendship* to the neglect of apostolate, discernment and obedience. Without a very conscious *apostolic* orientation, a group can become introverted, self-centered, 'cozy,' and even sentimental in its 'togetherness.' Without genuine *discernment*, relationships can remain superficial, unchallenged or naturalistic. Or community 'discussions' can become 'ego-trips' of self-revelation for the sake of 'personal growth' in a very diminished sense of the word....Without *obedience*, a group can lose its vital sense of mission, and thereby become isolated from a lively consciousness of its role in the mission of the universal Society. No matter how many lay-people of whichever sex such a group has in for dinner or days, it has become a fundamentally 'closed' community. At the extreme, its breadth of vision can have narrowed to a kind of solipsism.[1]

In a real community one needs not only the freedom to go his own way and the support of a genuinely expressed brotherhood, but also the challenge to walk ever further along the narrow path of the gospel, a path which is none other than Christ himself. That same longing which brings us together in community points farther than the other person, farther than friendship, farther than community, farther even than death. That longing has a tremendous, a truly infinite depth, namely God himself, who is the deepest Ground of both the individual and the group. In one of his plays Claudel has a woman say to her lover: "I am a promise that cannot be kept and that, precisely, makes me a grace." A woman loved and in love is a promise which evokes vast expectations, more than she can ever fulfill. She points beyond herself, therefore, to Ore who alone can fill to capacity the desires of a human heart. Restless is our heart till it finds its rest in God, said St.

Augustine. Chesterton said it more simply: "Even at home I am homesick."

True love and friendship are always open, referring beyond themselves. In this sense it has rightly been said that man can be a sacrament for the encountering of God. But then we must keep the perspective open so that God is indeed sought and can be found. It is only through our fellowmen that God comes to us; and it is only through God that men become truly fellowmen. The deepest expectation can be filled only by God. A community, therefore, is always in process, always on the way, and as such, it is a blessing. But then we must not block this perspective. May God incarnate render our hearts human enough so that with us our brothers may feel at home; may he make them pure enough so that with us our brothers may also feel at home with God.

Nineteen

UNMARRIAGEABLE FOR GOD'S SAKE

The Old Testament often speaks of virginity, but always the reference is to the virginity of the people as a whole; e.g., Jeremiah says, "I build you once more; you shall be rebuilt, virgin of Israel" (31:4), and again, "Come home, virgin of Israel, come home to these towns of yours" (31:21). In Isaiah we find the same concept: the chosen people as a whole is the virgin bride of Yahweh:

> Like a young man marrying a virgin
> so will the one who built you wed you,
> and as the bridegroom rejoices in his bride,
> so will your God rejoice in you (62:5).

> For now your creator will be your husband,
> his name, Yahweh Sabaoth;
> your redeemer will be the Holy One of Israel,
> he is called the God of the whole earth (54:5).

We can make the general statement that in the Old Testament virginity is never lived in a personal way. On the contrary, personal virginity is far removed from the mind of an Israelite. Fertility was a blessing, and the commandment of Genesis (1:28) "Be fruitful, multiply, fill the earth" was very sacred to the Jews.

The natural longing for posterity found in all people, but especially in more primitive people, was deepened to a far greater degree for the Israelite by the fact that the messiah had been promised as one of his race. To the Jews, therefore, the role of father and mother became sacred in a heightened sense. They had many sayings which illustrated their convictions in this matter; e.g., "Who does not marry is like a person who sheds blood," or "...is like a murderer!" A person who did not marry had the power of life within him but did not transmit it. Even as late as prophetic times Jeremiah's celibacy was a shock. The most striking example of this sacredness of parenthood is found in the Book of Judges (11:30-40), where we read the story of the daughter of Jephthah, who was to die for a mistaken and unlawful interpretation of a vow made by her father. She accepts her death submissively, but for the young girl, even worse than the death itself to which she is condemned is the fact that she must die without having been fruitful. "Grant me one request," she pleads, "let me be free for two months. I shall go and wander in the mountains, and with my companions bewail my virginity." The whole longing of the Israelite for children is heard in that plea, as it is also in the words of Rachel: "Give me children or I shall die" (Gen 30:1).

It is only in the New Testament that personal celibacy becomes a factor in human life. This is most probably connected with the incarnation and demonstrates that only an incarnate God can enable us to live as celibates, since it is the person of Jesus Christ who is at the heart of celibacy. Virginity can be realized only because of Christ and with him since it is only a continuous focusing on him which enables us to persevere in purity of heart and flesh without becoming turned in on ourselves. Matthew lists three categories of eunuchs:

Unmarriageable for God's Sake

> There are eunuchs born that way from their mother's womb, there are eunuchs made so by men and there are eunuchs who have made themselves that way for the sake of the kingdom of heaven. Let anyone accept this who can (19:12).

Because "eunuch" is such a horrible word, it is a very humbling experience to dwell upon the reality of this mystery. A eunuch is one who is incapable of human marriage. The very starkness of the phrase is in one way the highlight of all considerations of the mystery of celibacy. "Eunuch" sounds so much like "freak," an incomplete person, one somehow lacking an essential that constitutes him human. It intensifies the harshness of the truth which the word "virgin" softens somewhat. On the surface, to "make myself unmarriageable" seems to imply that I should make myself as unattractive as possible so that no one will be interested even in looking at me. But that would be a shallow and exterior approach to being unmarriageable. A more valid understanding of the mystery of celibacy would be this: A woman, very much in love with her husband, would have eyes for no other man. In this sense, she is no longer marriageable for any other man. She is bound and committed to this one alone—freely, happily. The real mystery of consecrated celibacy lies in the reason for it, expressed by Christ in the words "for the sake of the kingdom of heaven." The kingdom is where God truly reigns, where the will of God is fulfilled entirely; in other words, where God is fully God. In the history of salvation the kingdom of God so far has been fully realized only in Jesus Christ and in his mother Mary. In the person of Jesus, God's Will was totally accomplished; he *is* the kingdom of God enfleshed. From his time onward, celibacy for the kingdom of heaven is possible because

243

now it can find inspiration and impetus from contemplation of the kingdom as shaped in Jesus Christ. This is another way of saying that Jesus himself is at the heart of New Testamental celibacy.

In its final analysis, celibacy means being captured by Christ. He is our life (Col 3:4), fascinating us so completely that eventually we become unmarriageable. In its deepest sense, this is what celibacy means. It is *not* on the basis of pros and cons that one undertakes freely to live one's entire life in celibacy, nor is it just a state of being unmarried; rather, it is existentially being incapable of marriage. When Jesus says there are eunuchs that have made themselves thus for the sake of the kingdom of heaven, he is pointing out that true celibacy is achieved not in a single leap, but by a process of slow growth. The Rule of Taizé says, "This work of Christ in you demands infinite patience." When a person takes first or even final vows, usually he is not yet unmarriageable. What he expresses in his vow is a two-fold covenant: he professes publicly for everyone to know that he recognizes as an ideal for himself the state of being unmarriageable for the sake of the kingdom of heaven; and he promises that he will put forth every effort to achieve this goal. He will not try to preserve himself marriageable as long as possible; on the contrary, he will try seriously, honestly to make himself unmarriageable. It is a long, sometimes difficult road to become unmarriageable for the sake of the kingdom. It can take years, even decades, to progress far on this narrow way of being fascinated by Jesus Christ, but by his vow the religious promises to advance as quickly as he can. He will not procrastinate. This is his ideal, and he will run to meet it. Only when the point of really being unmarriageable has been reached has celibacy become fully mature. In a book written for priests, *La Peur ou la Foi*, Maurice Bellet has observed: Suppose one morning a priest reads in his newspaper that the Pope has changed his mind on the Encyclical *Sacerdotalis celibatus*; from now on celibacy will be optional for priests. If that priest at this point has to make up his mind what he is going to do—make use of the new opening for marriage or remain celibate—the mere fact that he has to deliberate indicates that he is not yet existentially unmarriageable. Thus far, he is only juridically unmarriageable. Genuine celibacy goes so much deeper than a law because it is the interiorization of the goal of that law.[1]

The content of celibacy is eminently positive. It involves not just being unmarried, but being fascinated by another—Christ—to such a degree that marriage is no longer possible. Celibacy does not mean that one has lost something, but rather that the celibate has found Someone. In essence, celibacy is love which can no longer wait; that is what makes it fruitful. There is another dimension, at once ecclesial and eschatological, which enhances the value of celibacy and helps to prevent it from becoming myopic or introspective. The celibate stands as an enduring witness that all Christians are pledged to a new order of grace, the fullness of which is that kingdom where no one will be given in marriage. He thus becomes by his celibacy a prophetic voice, recalling to all men that there are ultimate values not wholly attainable in our present life, and that it is only at our journey's end that we shall experience the fullness of God's giving. En route, there is only one thing necessary: God's love as revealed in Christ. Celibacy is a pilgrimage, a tremendous adventure. Along this way we meet magnificent people who have really become unmarriageable because of God. Unhappily, we also meet some who in their celibacy have not come to complete fulfillment, but have become bogged down along the road.

There is a danger, of course, a risk involved in celibacy because there we lack the incentives provided by marriage and the care of a family. This means that celibacy can lead to a coldness of heart, a lack of affection, possibly even to laziness. The only radical remedy against this danger is to focus all our attention on the heart and inspiration of celibacy, for unless it is based on deep attraction for the person of Christ, celibacy can be irresponsible. In this lies its real challenge. It would be unrealistic to ignore the fact that the celibate life involves a genuine deprivation, something which we miss because we are celibates. Jesus answered the man who wanted to follow him wherever he went: "Foxes have holes and the birds of the air have nests, but the Son of Man has nowhere to lay his head" (Lk 9:58). So, no home of his own for the Son of Man, no home of his own for the celibate! One who follows Christ in the celibate way has no conjugal ties—no husband or wife or children—and he misses the warmth these can provide and the appeal they can make on him. This is the negative element in celibacy. There is also a positive element: viz., the fascination which Christ has for this person, the dedication to the apostolate or to contemplative life, the commitment to the kingdom of God, the being available for the people of God.

In every celibate life both the positive and the negative elements are always present, but in varying degrees, and in this lies the differing quality of celibacy. We call that a negative celibacy when the negative element predominates even though there is, of course, some minor positive element present. The first impression this type of celibacy gives is a kind of frustration, a deprivation; something is missing. We speak about a positive celibacy when—the negative element being present to a certain degree—the over-all impression is that of a wholesome life at once fulfilled and appealing.

It is the celibacy in which negative elements prevail which presents the greatest difficulty, yet its problems are not ineradicable. There is always possible a genuine conversion which will transmute the negative, making it genuinely positive. This conversion may require that the religious relinquish some things in order to find Christ and to contemplate him more deeply so that he may fill the emptiness. Perhaps there is some foreign element blocking Christ's way in the life of negative celibacy, and until this is removed, the joy of positive celibacy remains elusive. It is important that there be a genuine transformation of this negative celibacy into a positive one, a transformation that is truly worth the price it exacts.

There is a second way to cope with negative celibacy: to seek dispensation from the vows and then to leave in order to search for happiness elsewhere.

Apart from these two radical ways to overcome negative celibacy, there are also two forms of compromise open. In these methods of temporizing the celibate does not break his promise by giving up his vows, nor does he take the radical measure to make his celibacy really positive, but he seeks the in-between solutions of either sublimation or compensation.

— In sublimation the gap which is there and which is predominant is filled up with important human values. In themselves, of course, these human values were not the reason why the religious chose celibacy, but having more or less failed in the option he did choose, he tries to make the best of the situation by sublimating it into human values which in themselves are good: work, relations with others, influential positions, broad culture, wide interests. The pain of not being able to marry, of not being father or mother, is assuaged to some extent by these other values. People attempting this sublimation work very hard; they frequently carry almost a double load, and others may marvel at their efficiency and their energy. Outwardly, their life seems anything but a failure. And yet, deep down, this celibacy is a failure because it was never intended for this excessive work-load. Or such a person may seek out many social contacts and relationships, many friends. Or it may be a devotion to study or a drive for power which pre-empts his attention. In all this, the reaction is a sublimation of the real core of celibacy.

— The other type of compromise for coping with negative celibacy without abandoning it completely or transforming it to the positive is compensation, basically the same substitution of a lesser value for the real one, but here the human values used to fill the gap are no longer important ones, but rather of a lower species: insipid literature, curiosity, shallow hobbies.

Neither of these ways out of negative celibacy—sublimation or compensation—is a sufficiently radical solution to the problem. The only effective way to combat negative celibacy is to grow into positive celibacy, that is to strengthen the positive element by means of a deeper, more intent focusing on the kingdom of heaven incarnate in Jesus.

Since the deepest root and inspiration of true celibacy is the person of Christ, the people of God also play an important role in celibacy, and this in two ways:

dedication to the kingdom of heaven always means dedication to the body of Christ as formed by the people; and celibacy needs the support of the people of God and, even more pointedly, the support of the community. Celibacy is not constituted by turning away from the people; rather it is constituted by the fact that through the celibate God turns himself towards the people. A celibate is not divided, torn between Christ and the people. He lets his affection for the people coincide as completely as possible with Christ's love for them because he is taken up in this covenant relation between God and his people. Thus, a person who gives himself to Christ gives himself to the Christ who offered himself for everybody; therefore, genuine dedication to Christ is always dedication to all whom we encounter. In fact, celibacy always implies the call to devote oneself to the neighbor with Christ's own love. If we really give ourselves to Christ, he will enlarge our hearts so that we can embrace many and live truly fruitful lives.

This dedication to Christ, however, is lived in the darkness of faith and the longing of hope, and often the fruitfulness of our lives is not apparent. We commit ourselves to Christ, but we have never seen him. We have to live with a certainty that has no basis in this visible world; there is no hand to hold. The man who lives thus is brave and mature: no one who has seen this or who has tried it himself will deny that. A celibate life is a courageous life, one that has a kind of poverty about it because it offers nothing tangible to which I can cling. I can never grasp God. Sociologically, the poverty of celibacy is often looked upon as something to be pitied. This can be a grace to be exploited—one that the celibate would betray if he sought to create an impression of heroism before the people. Instead of trying to elevate celibacy to a pedestal, let him live it as one of the poor of Yahweh:

> You have seduced me, Yahweh, and I have let myself be seduced:
> you have overpowered me: you were the stronger.
> I am a daily laughing-stock,
> everybody's butt (Jer 20:7).

In some of our recent theologizing it is possible that we cross the narrow line between giving reasons for the hope that is within us and giving proof for the validity of our way of life. Underlying this is the sometimes barely acknowledged desire to make ourselves important to ourselves.

Nor should the celibate claim that his celibacy makes him completely available to the people because such a claim would be too pretentious, giving him an honor which he does not deserve. Celibacy for the sake of the kingdom of heaven does not need anything outside itself to justify it. In itself it is a service, provided that it is lived to the full. The ultimate service I render is not that I have more time, that I am more free for people, but that I have pledged as my most constant ideal openness to God and the public testimony of the reality of God in my life. Celibacy is not to be admired by the people. All that is important is that I should be captured by Christ and spread the news of his love. It is enough that religious be a "light to the world," a beacon to travelers, not so much something for people to admire, as a light by which they see the direction in which they are to go. The very simplicity in which we live our celibacy can in itself be a sign which silently and humbly promotes the reality of God. This is the greatest service we can render to people by our celibacy—to show them that God is so real that he can truly fill a human heart and can bring a human life to fulfillment. Cardinal Suhard says: "To be a witness does not consist in engaging in propaganda nor even in stirring up people, but in being a living mystery. It means to live in such a way that one's life would not make sense if God did not exist."

There is a final way in which other people enter into our celibacy: for a truly celibate life we need the support of others. A cold community which affectively isolates a celibate can do great harm to the growth of positive celibacy in its members. We can never come to God completely by ourselves; we need the inspiration and affection of our fellowmen. It is not that we should claim that support or demand it; that is a most sure way of ruining it. But we should be able to hope for it. And we certainly should be poor and humble enough to be receptive to it when it is freely and purely given. This means that the people in the parish are partly responsible for the celibacy of their priests, and members of a religious community have mutually promised to be responsible for one another's celibacy. We are to be living signs of God's love. Celibacy would be a mere caricature of the gospel if it did not make visible God's love in the human community: "See how they love one another!"

Twenty

A SENSE OF MISSION

If we want truly to understand what obedience in the religious life means, we must first clear away those caricatures of obedience which have emerged in the course of centuries and have blurred its real content.

There is, first of all, the attempt to identify the obedience of a religious with that of a child. We must be absolutely clear about this: religious obedience has no connection with that which children owe to their parents. The obedience of children necessarily becomes superfluous as the child advances—this is its whole intent—whereas religious obedience is something promised for a lifetime. The obedience of a child presupposes that the child must still be educated, and the purpose of his obedience is precisely to bring the child to that point of maturity where it can handle its own life independently. But religious obedience presupposes that one has already been educated. It implies also that the superior is not necessarily wiser or more experienced than the one who obeys. If this were the case, we would again be establishing an educational relationship between the superior and the religious, a relationship that obviously is out of place. In fact, religious obedience is possible only for mature persons. The petty person will always try—and usually succeed—to find a way out, but the mature person is prepared to face difficulties unafraid since he knows he can never really lose his true self. In our time Teilhard de Chardin probably stands out as the example par excellence of a man who by the very maturity of his natural and supernatural make-up was able to obey in the heroic way which gave to his life the fruitfulness of the grain of wheat that died in the ground.

Another misrepresentation depicts religious obedience as an efficient way to run the community, a kind of traffic regulation for those living and working together, a sensible way for sensible people to share their common life and its arrangements. This side-effect, of course, may be a certain result of obedience, but that can never be its whole purpose. Religious obedience along this line is attained only when our common concern deepens to the level of mystery, when we really form one community, one body, the body of Christ, whose food is the Will of the Father.

A third caricature is the mistaking of servile obedience for genuine religious obedience. Servile obedience seeks to please the human person of the superior or to win the approval of the one in charge. This type of obedience pedestals the opinions, desires, likes of the superior, making all genuine exchange of ideas and thoughts impossible. It is a degrading corruption of obedience, one that can be caused either by the superior who desires to hear no opinion or inspiration not agreeing with his, or by the religious who, having a servile, immature nature, lacks the strength of character to form his own opinions.

A fourth caricature of obedience comprises those socio-psychological structures belonging to past eras—feudal, monarchic, totalitarian, or centralist—which exacted a kind of obedience corresponding to their prevailing philosophies. Just as there is a type of man who seems to require a certain type of authority, so there is, conversely, a type of authority which creates its own type of man. When religious life remains dominated by antiquated types of authority, true religious obedience will thereby be thwarted. Under this heading we can include also that kind of obedience which flows only from the top down, without any serious input from below.

A final caricature of obedience understands it as an ascetical means, one that will help to break stubborn wills and lead to humility. But obedience for the sake of obedience is an artificial, inauthentic way to humility. It produces only a debasing servility, a meticulous, even ridiculous dependence, a dull carrying out of orders, a willingness to let others think for us rather than to do our own thinking.

None of these caricatures, obviously, constitutes that sanctifying and strengthening response which is the object of the vow of religious obedience. Genuine obedience has completely different roots since it is based on a passion for the Will of God; it flows from the conviction that God is love and that what God wants us to do is always for our good, yes even for our greatest good. God is the deepest Ground of our being, and to act according to his Will is the only way authentically to unfold ourselves, to become more and more the persons we really are and the community we are meant to form. That is why the scriptures always present obedience as the source of man's fruitfulness and joy. Obedience to the word of God here and now is not a confining of our being; rather it is the only way to achieve our completion. The Will of God is identical with his love; this means that it is both life-giving and liberating. God wants every person, all peoples to live and to be thoroughly happy. He is no threat either to man or to mankind; on the contrary, it is only in surrender to God that man comes to his complete unfolding and the world to its full fruition. Outside the realm of God's Will there is no apostolate, no service to others possible. If there was one message which Christ reiterated untiringly and with growing urgency it was this: his life with all the inspiration it gives was rooted wholly in the Will of the Father: "My food is to do the will of the one who sent me, and to complete his work" (Jn 4:34). ". . .my aim is to do not my own will, but the will of him who sent me" (Jn 5:30). ". . .I have come from heaven not to do my own will, but to do the will of the one who sent me" (Jn 6:38). "He who sent me is with me, and has not left me to myself, for I always do what pleases him" (Jn 8:29).

We can see, therefore, that Jesus conceived his life wholly in these terms: it was a mission entrusted to him by his Father. And religious obedience is the extension of that mission:

> As the Father sent me,
> so I am sending you (Jn 20:21).

"In your minds you must be the same as Christ Jesus" (Phil 2:5). Religious obedience is not only centered on the person of Christ; it tries to continue the heart of his life. It is the continuation of, the participation in the obedience of Christ himself; through him we say our *yes* to God (2 Cor 1:20). It is like an identification with Christ, a becoming transparent so that the basic inspiration of Christ's life may shine through.

The word *obedience* comes from the Latin *ob-audire*, to listen intensely. In the case of religious obedience it means to listen intensely to the voice of God in order to act upon his word. In this way we live a responsible life, i.e., we make our life into a response.

A Sense of Mission

It is difficult, obviously, to discover what God really desires or wills in our lives. The glibness with which some people speak about the Will of God is almost blasphemous at times. When a child is killed in a car accident caused by an intoxicated driver, it would be sacrilegious to say that God willed this. And some superiors may well have been guilty for imposing as God's Will what was really their own wish or inclination. To search out this divine Will can be a slow, difficult enterprise, one for which we need the help and sustaining power of each other. It is the Christian belief that God's first word is to his people, to the group as a whole, and to individuals as members of this people. Thus the human community is involved in the discovery of God's Will. In a sense, this intertwining of the human and the divine elements in religious obedience constitutes a prolongation of the incarnation. Christ incarnate is a person who is at the same time completely divine and completely human. In the sacraments there is a true prolongation of this symbiosis of the divine and the human, for there too we have human realities with a divine core. E.g., confession is a human dialogue between a person verbalizing his guilt and another person absolving that guilt. But we know that no one can forgive sins save God alone. The human communication in confession, therefore, contains a divine element. Likewise in the Eucharist we have a human celebration in which we read and listen, pray and sing, and then offer and consecrate and receive bread and wine. But we believe that in this celebration the bread is transformed into the body of Christ so that the human celebration reaches a divine depth. Religious obedience involves this same kind of prolongation of the incarnation, less intense, to be sure, but no less real. There too we have a human dialogue—

sometimes all too human—and in this encounter the Will of God is found.

The heart of obedience is that it is a human way, an authentic human way to discover the Will of God. This is true both in communal obedience, where the whole community as such tries to discover this Will, and in individual obedience, where an individual with his superior tries to hear the word of God. The same basic pattern is evident in both. The first stage of this pattern is that the individual or the individual members of the community try to discover for themselves in faith and prayer what God is saying. Even in those cases where the initial proposal or request comes from the superior, this personal consideration and investigation are the first stage of obedience. This stage presupposes the genuine desire not only to know God's Will but also unconditionally to carry it out. Anyone refusing to commit himself beforehand has already erected a barrier to finding God's Will. When a person first wants to know God's Will and only then will decide whether or not he will carry it out, he does not give the right preponderance to the Will of God. This first stage also presupposes an inner freedom, which means that I am capable of doing the exact opposite of what I had planned or hoped for and that I am willing to do so. When this inner freedom is lacking, rationalization will ensue, in which the person will think his own will is God's Will. To distinguish authentically between the word of God and the voice of my own self-will or selfishness requires both prayer and abnegation. It may require patience too, but above all, it requires deep sincerity and inner detachment.

In the second stage of obedience I convey what I think is God's word in the situation to the group or to the superior. The verbalization of what I have found often leads to a consciencization and also a purification of my own discovery. As long as I keep what I think is God's word within my own heart or mind, I can still distort the picture, over-emphasize a certain aspect. But when I speak to others, a certain balance is effected. I have to make serious efforts in order to be certain that the other person or persons understand correctly what I have seen, nor can I rest until I am convinced that this is so. It is possible that I shall need more than one session for this dialogue since the second stage will be fulfilled only when I am sure that the superior or the group truly knows what I understand in conscience about the particular issue.

The third and the decisive stage of obedience is the most mature: I leave the final decision to the superior or to the community who through the mouth of the superior tells me what to do. I have made my own contribution to the full, and through our common dialogue it has been integrated into the greater knowledge and insight of the superior or the group as a whole. After this integration I may receive my own idea back, but now it is different; it is commissioned by religious authority. I am no longer led by my own convictions alone, but I am sent by the Church, as it were, in the continuation of Christ's mission by the Father. It may happen that the voice of authority of the group or the superior changes my contribution wholly or in part. My inspiration may have been modified by its integration into the wider, higher view of authority. The community or the superior knows what I know because I have intimated this to them; they may also know more than I, and that greater knowledge or insight may change the impact of my contribution. It is here that our faith that God's word comes to and through the community becomes concrete and effective. Also, in this case I receive my mission—different from what I myself may have understood—through the community as a prolongation of the mission of Christ. To this mission and to the certainty it entails, I have a right since the community accepted my vow of obedience.

Because it requires in a concrete and specific way that we transcend our own individualism, this third stage can be difficult, demanding great maturity and generosity. At the same time it can also be very beautiful when both the individual and the authority are really open, are not pressing their own views determinedly. Pressure on one side will inevitably create counter-pressure on the other, which will do fatal harm to the authentic search for and discovery of God's Will. When there is a sincere willingness not to cling to one's own insights and to let loose what one has found, obedience will be a sacred happening, and both partners will experience the presence of God and the deep peace this always brings. This is not to deny the pain that can be involved in obedience, for it may well be that the intervention of the voice of authority constitutes a refusal of what I had sincerely thought to be God's Will. Without this intervention, however, there is no religious obedience, no extension of the mission of Christ. When authority speaks too early, we have dictatorship; when it speaks too late, we have indecisiveness, and disrupting confusion will follow. It is obvious that both partners must be supernatural people or the dialogue will be cast in ambiguity and doomed to failure. When there is a sincere search for the Will of God and an unconditional readiness to fulfill that will, when an atmosphere of faith and prayerfulness and openness prevails, then religious obedience is the most seasoned, most complete way to discover the all-important Will of God.

Twenty-One

COMMISSIONED TO A NEW NEED

The attempt to clarify the meaning of religious life today involves the inherent risk of rendering that life self-focused. Religious life is lived by well over a million people throughout the world. We cannot say that all of them are happy or have reached fulfillment, but neither can we say that most of them are unhappy. Religious life is always a risk, an adventure. It can, and sometimes does fail although for many it provides fulfillment and the possibility of service and sincere community life, which leads to a genuine personal unfolding. This proves that religious life is meaningful. Since life itself is prior to reflection—*ortho-praxis* comes before *ortho-doxia*—we shall find the essential meaning of religious life only in living it. E.g., there is little point in living in an affluent way while, at the same time, discussing and searching endlessly for the meaning of poverty; we shall never find it. Nor is there anything to be gained by living the third way and then asking for a deeper sense of celibacy. Again it is only in living it that the true value of celibacy can be discovered.

However, even while the true perspective of religious life is found in living it, we still have to express its essence in words, and this for several reasons:

— It is a valid human desire to want to perceive the meaning of one's life.

— It is a help to live religious life with greater dedication and conviction when one has a clear insight into its meaning.

— Clarity on the meaning of religious life is a genuine help in the renewal, where those who have only a vague concept of what religious life really is tend to become either a brake, resisting any change, or a windbag, going along with any novelty.

— For some religious the identity crisis has provoked deep pain and suffering, so there is a great deal of human happiness involved in expressing the deeper meaning of the religious life.

— Secularization forces us to answer the core question: what is the difference between a religious and a lay person? Since so many of the external differences have disappeared, the basic difference becomes all the more vital.

At Vatican II many prolonged, really fervent discussions took place concerning the place of religious in the Church. The background of these discussions was the concept of the double vocation, the two-fold way of living the gospel. This had been the common doctrine in the past: there was a way of the commandments, which ordinary Christians would follow, and there was the way of the counsels, which religious would take. After vehement discussion the doctrine of the double way has been abandoned by Vatican II, which stressed that in the last analysis there is only one Christian vocation, and that it is impossible to add anything over and above this call of Christ. This decision coincides well with the existential conviction of modern man, both lay and religious. We religious desire to know ourselves one with Christians in the world, not apart from them, let alone above them. We want to live a way of life very close to that of lay people, and consequently we are strongly averse to any artificial differences in life-style. Also we think that the way of the commandments is basically the route that all must follow, and he who fulfills these ten commandments really comes to perfection. Perhaps the way of the commandments is actually the way of only two commandments: to love the Lord our God with all our heart and all our soul and all our strength and to love our neighbor as ourself. We understand clearly that these two commandments are so demanding that we shall never really fulfill them, let alone add a greater dimension and accomplish even more than they ask. The contemporary religious acknowledges that since there is only one religious vocation, the religious is animated by the same inspiration that all believing Christians know. It is the baptismal grace as the root of religious life which we desire to see stressed: "For the foundation, nobody can lay any other than the one which has already been laid, that is Jesus Christ" (1 Cor 3:11). We do not see ourselves as the only ones trying to live faith in Christ and to give it shape in this world, nor do we think that we realize this goal in the best or the most perfect way. It is the unity of all Christians, lay people and religious, which we want to emphasize, for all Christians have only one path on which to journey—the narrow path which is Christ himself.

In spite of this fundamental unity between religious and lay persons, however, there is still a certain difference although it is difficult to express clearly just wherein the distinction can be found. We religious carry as a mark on our forehead that which each Christian lives and guards in his heart as his deepest, most precious mystery. We are all animated by the same inspiration, but in religious life this is expressed publicly so that everyone can see that we belong to Christ both now and for eternity. It is made visible in us so that our whole life becomes an expression of that to which the gospel calls all Christians. In this way our life constitutes a visible sign, a witness and an inspiration. It is not that we are a sign by the way we dress nor even by what we say or do, but rather by what we are. The life we lead is inexplicable without faith in Jesus Christ, who is, of course, the corner-stone, the only foundation for any Christian. One notices this when one talks intimately with a believing Christian. This has been one of the great discoveries of my priesthood. I had known that lay people were fervent in their faith and in the living of it, but it was only after my ordination that I learned how fervent and how generous they often are. After I had been introduced as a priest into the hidden chambers of their hearts, I was able to see this and to experience a joy and inspiration far beyond anything I had anticipated.

Now in the matter of the distinction between the lay and the religious state this is exactly the crux: faith and dedication to Christ are strong and spirited in lay people, having a tremendous, an ultimate value for them, but only an intimate can know how true this is; whereas a religious expresses what Christ means to him by the very structure of his life. The whole Church embodies the evangelical counsels, but in a religious they become publicly visible and tangible. The religious makes particular that which is general in the Church, giving it a name and a public, external expression. The vows are not just means for living a Christian life; they are also a specific expression of that life. Religious life is a state which from a merely secular point of view does not make perfect sense. In other words, the state of life comprising celibacy, poverty, and obedience, cannot be fully understood unless through faith; therefore by their very life-style and their state, religious express openly how indispensable faith is to the meaning of their lives. They live in such a way that their lives would make no sense if God did not exist, or more positively, they show that God is real and can bring a human life to fulfillment. In this way they show forth more explicitly what lives in every Christian. In this lies the prophetic charism of religious life. This is the reason why lay people can be so disappointed in religious who fail in their vocation because the deepest and most cherished mystery of the life of lay people has been entrusted to us religious in a special way. When our religious life fails, their ideal is damaged. We are theirs; in a very deep sense we belong to the lay people. This does not mean merely that we must be available to help them in their daily needs. On a far deeper level we give expression to their faith—and that is our truly responsible mission.

In a herd at times one animal is marked with a branding iron on its forehead to indicate that this herd belongs to a particular owner. There is no need to brand each individual animal; one will suffice for the whole herd. It does not mean that only the branded animal belongs to the owner; all the animals are his. What is true for all is expressed through the branded one. But then, of course, it is necessary that this branded animal remain in the herd.

There are a few significant consequences of this view on religious life. The sign, the witnessing, will not always be understood. If that were the case and if there were no ambiguity involved, it would not truly be a sign. In other words, a certain amount of being misunderstood, of being misjudged, is inseparable from religious life. When we accept the call of Christ to this state of life, we must accept also the likelihood that we shall be socially compromised by our association with Christ:

Remember the words I said to you:
A servant is not greater than his master.
If they persecuted me,
they will persecute you too (Jn 15:20).

Nor is this contempt only to be anticipated from non-Christians or from non-religious. "A man's enemies will be those of his own household" (Mt 10:36).

A sign should not disappear into its background. If I paint a fence with a certain color, it is senseless for me to paint an arrow of the same color on this fence. White on white may provide an interesting artistic experiment; it is worthless as a directional aid. A religious, obviously, should not do the extraordinary for the extraordinary's sake; on the other hand, he should make certain that he does live the essentials of his religious life and distinguish himself in that. In line with the thinking of Vatican II we must eliminate from our lives as religious all peculiarities which are merely forms of living in the past. At the same time we have to deepen the strangeness of being authentic religious, of living poverty, celibacy, obedience to the full. Often for religious in an identity crisis the problem is not so much poverty as lack of poverty; not so much celibacy, as lack of celibacy; just as a lack of obedience creates greater problems than obedience itself. We have to live in such a way that indeed we do witness to our vows. When we are no longer a sign, we shall become a scandal. In another context Edward Farrell has quoted Karl Rahner who developed this kind of failure tersely:

Rahner makes a rather frightening statement in one of the dictionaries of dogmatic theology. He writes that atheism can be created by someone preaching the gospel who does not believe in it. He said in addition that this is not uncommon....The Christian bears responsibility or culpability in creating atheism by mouthing that which he does not live.[1]

We have to accept the limitations of our life-style. Religious life is just *a way* to follow Christ; it is not the *only way*. Because the life-style of religious is a limited one, we should not try to introduce into it all kinds of values precious in their own right but foreign to our state of life. It would be immature to seek to assimilate or to take as one's own everything that may seem worthwhile. We must have the wisdom to acknowledge the good of certain things without desiring them for ourselves. Each of the vows demands the sacrifice of an important human value, yet it is in that sacrifice that we express how much the love of God and the dedication to Christ and to his kingdom mean to us. Therefore, we must be on guard against a tendency to accumulate that which may stifle the deepest inspiration of our lives:

> Enter by the narrow gate, since the road that leads to perdition is wide and spacious, and many take it; but it is a narrow gate and a hard road that leads to life, and only a few find it (Mt 7:13-14).

Obviously, we should not disdain those values which do not agree with our state of life. "Everything God has created is good" (1 Tim 4:4). On the other hand, we should not yield to the immature egoism that seeks to eat its cake and have it.

In this difficult service we need each other in the mutual support of the community. Community life requires of us:

— a great respect for the uniqueness of each person. We must give the others scope and freedom to be themselves;

— a mutual challenge to tread the narrow path to which the gospel calls us. We have to give each other the service of this challenge.

To put this in a negative way: there are those who have left religious life because they have felt stifled in it, not having the liberty to be themselves. For them the first element, respect for their uniqueness, was lacking. But there have been others who have left because the second element was missing: they found so much mediocrity, so much comfort and lack of religious inspiration, that the genuine appeal needed to live religious life was lacking and they could no longer persevere in their vocation.

It is obvious that we should never try to be a sign merely for the sake of being a sign because that would be inauthentic. In the last analysis, we do not want to be a sign; our ultimate concern is Jesus Christ himself. It is because of him that we are called to this way of life. The sign-element is only secondary.

There is a remarkable parallel between the recent historical and sociological evolution of religious life and the new theological interpretation of its meaning. The last century of church history records the foundations of many communities of men and women, at whose cradle there seems to have been the common element of keen awareness of the needs of the people, needs to which the rest of society seemed blind. The people who founded these communities perceived these needs so clearly, how-ever, that they were impelled to do something about them. They dedicated themselves, therefore, with tremendous generosity to teaching the poor, nursing the sick, caring for orphans, bringing Christ to foreign lands. The records of good accomplished are impressive, but perhaps the greatest achievement is that each community managed to communicate an awareness of these needs to society at large. After witnessing decades of this uncompromising dedication, the eyes of a country or a nation were opened. Gradually the education of the poor, nursing the sick, care of orphans, etc., were taken over as a public responsibility. It is to the credit of the religious communities that they pioneered in these services.

But if the old needs which still exist can be taken over by others—and I think that there are few services now rendered by religious which cannot be fulfilled by lay people—is there a new need to which religious life may dedicate itself? More specifically, is there a future for religious life? As I see it, the greatest need of our day is the need for faith. For too many people, it is hard to believe. They wrestle with such questions as: Is there a life after death? Has prayer any sense or is it merely a sophisticated form of introspection? What about the Eucharist? What can one believe of the bible? Does God exist at all, or is he merely a projection of an anxious human heart? I do not mean to say that faith was easy in the past, nor do I want to give the impression that previous centuries were permeated with genuine, lively faith. But I do think that the general atmosphere of the society took faith more for granted as a common and obvious value than it is willing to do today, and as a result supported the faith of the individuals more readily than it does today.

This crisis of faith has far-reaching consequences. It touches immediately the meaningfulness of life, which is a vital question; for when life has no purpose or no value, any suffering is too great and despair is much more prevalent than in a society where existence is meaningful.

— When faith is weak or absent, loneliness becomes a far greater threat. In a culture imbued by faith people can seek solitude because they can find God there, and people have always done so. But when God is dead, solitude becomes lonesomeness, and people must gather and talk together to drive away their sense of loneliness. There seems more talking now than ever before, but perhaps less real contact!

— When there is neither faith nor a sense of the spiritual, their lack can lead to an excessive emphasis on busyness and achievements so that a work-oriented culture arises in place of a God-oriented one. Again this means much suffering: first of all, of course, for those unable to work or no longer able to do so, for they feel like nobodies, frustrated and ignored. But also to those who can and do work this orientation can bring much misery. How many marriages have been destroyed because one or both partners sacrificed their marriage to a career? And how many religious have lost the original inspiration of their vocation because it was stifled by too heavy a work-load?

— When the spirit of faith and prayer weakens, the Church loses something of its interior strength and inspiration. This in turn leads easily to an over-emphasis on the exterior, to a petrifying of structures and positions, which may cause unevangelical suffering to individuals and can do much harm to the credibility of the Church, thus reinforcing in a vicious circle the crisis of faith.

— The grave injustices in the world at large also have a close connection with the weakness of faith, and this in a two-fold direction: when faith is feeble, injustice grows and institutionalizes much more rapidly; and the lack of concern for injustices in the world on the part of those countries considered Christian makes faith utterly unacceptable to the non-Christian world.

If we religious have a future, it is in realizing this need here and now and dedicating ourselves to it. This means specifically that we must help people to believe and to pray. There is need for adult religious education, for prayer groups, for spiritual direction, and the like. Yet even these activities are not the first task that I have in mind; there is something more essential still. The real breakthrough in the crisis of faith and the repression of spirituality can be brought about only by ourselves praying and living the faith. More than in previous times, we need to concentrate on the essentials of the religious inspiration in living genuinely and obviously the vows we have taken and by being truly, deeply persons of prayer. This basic service of living the faith and thereby helping others to believe can be rendered while doing any type of job. I think we must distinguish between the primary service of religious, which is helping people to believe, and the secondary task, which is the particular apostolate in which we may happen to be engaged. There is, of course, genuine importance to the choice of the secondary task, but I am convinced that the primary service is far more important and can be realized in almost any of our secondary-level services.

This new task of religious life does not necessarily require large numbers. When the service rendered is the running of a large institution, we do need numbers. When the service is living the faith, we can do with small numbers, but in this latter situation, the basic values of the religious life must be stressed all the more. Our poverty, which is a real value and which we must live, will help people see that God does exist. If we can be happy with nothing, then we show that God is a reality and we help people to believe this. The same is true of celibacy. If we show that we can come to fulfillment by really dedicating ourselves to Jesus Christ, by making ourselves unmarriageable for his sake, this too is a sign which becomes a help for people. And what of our obedience? If it is not just a listening to what someone else is saying, an abdication of our own personal integrity—you don't have to think; they'll think for you—but a genuine attempt to discover the Will of God in utter openness and generosity, in interplay and surrender, then our obedience too is a genuine sign. All of this can be done only in prayer, which in itself is a witnessing in spite of itself.

This bird's-eye view of the recent developments in religious life leads to the same path for the religious of the future as we discovered in the first part of this chapter: to shed the oddness which reflects a culture alien to our own times and habits of thought and, at the same time, to reinforce the oddness of being men and women whose hearts are always poor and empty, hungry and thirsty, because of our passion for God. It requires courage to follow Jesus Christ, particularly since we can never follow him without experiencing that social disdain which is inevitable for his associates. We shall be compromised because in our society it is strange to be poor, celibate, obedient, prayerful. But if we water down these basic values so that our life becomes comfortable and just like the life everyone leads, then religious life will have lost its inner meaning. Or, to put it another way, when we make religious life so comfortable that we have everything we want, then there is no reason to leave; but then, there is no reason to enter either. It is at this nadir that we shall witness the demise of religious life.

What do I see? I see a small, radical band of people who really want to follow Christ with their whole heart. We find them in communities everywhere. They will be liked by the people because they are one with them and really belong to them. They are available—and yet, at the same time, they are strange, cannot be fully understood. They have a mystery which they carry within themselves and to which they witness. And they are happy in doing so. The people living that radical, incomprehensible life radiate joy—and they do "refer" to God. I believe that this is the mission of religious life today.

FOOTNOTES

Unless otherwise stated all biblical quotations are taken from *The Jerusalem Bible* (New York: Doubleday & Company, Inc., 1966). The abbreviation NAB refers to *The New American Bible* (New York: Benziger, 1970).

Chapter 3

[1]Quoted in Thomas A. Harris, M.D., *I'm OK— You're OK* (New York: Harper and Row, 1969), 236.

[2]Pierre Teilhard de Chardin, *Hymn of the Universe* (New York: Harper and Row, 1965), 34.

Chapter 5A

[1]Archbishop Anthony Bloom, *Living Prayer* (Springfield, Ill.: Templegate Publishers, 1966), 58.

Chapter 5B

[1]N.N., *Avontuur in Geloof, Hoop en Liefde* (Antwerpen: Patmos, 1965), 123.

Chapter 7

[1]Anthony Bloom, *Meditations* (Denville, N.J.: Dimension Books, 1972), 58-61 *passim.*

[2]Henri J. M. Nouwen, *The Wounded Healer* (Garden City, N.Y.: Doubleday & Co., 1972), 32-33. Riesman's article appeared in *Psychology Today*, October, 1969.

Chapter 9

[1]John C. Haughey, S.J., *The Conspiracy of God: The Holy Spirit in Men* (Garden City, N.Y.: Doubleday & Co., 1973), 7-8 and 11.

Footnotes

[2]Thomas Merton, *New Seeds of Contemplation* (New York: New Directions, 1961), 45.

[3]Haughey, *Conspiracy of God*, p. 6.

Chapter 10

[1]I owe some of these thoughts to a Dutch article by Bas van Iersel, a translation of which can be found in a book by the same author: *The Bible on the Temptations of Man* (De Pere, Wisc.: St. Norbert Abbey Press, 1966), 41-67.

[2]René Voillaume, *Lettres aux Fraternités* I (Paris: Cerf, 1960), 303; see English translation in *Brothers of Men* (Denville, N.J.: Dimension Books, 1972), 133.

[3]Ladislas M. Orsy, S.J., *Open to the Spirit* (Denville, N.J.: Dimension Books, 1970), 90-91.

[4]Haughey, *Conspiracy of God*, p. 36.

Chapter 12

[1]Catherine de Hueck Doherty, *Poustinia* (Notre Dame, Ind.: Ave Maria Press, 1975), 100.

[2]Adapted from Henri J. M. Nouwen, *Out of Solitude* (Notre Dame, Ind.: Ave Maria Press, 1974), 32-37, *passim.*

[3]Alexander Solzhenitsyn, *Poems*, translated by *Patricia Blake*, © 1972 by Patricia Blake.

Chapter 13

[1]Cf. Ann Wylder, S.C., "The Exercises and Maturity," in Supplement to *The Way*, No. 19, Summer, 1973, 28.

Chapter 18A

[1]Antoine de Saint-Exupéry, *The Little Prince* (New York: Reynal and Hitchcock, 1943), 64-72.

Footnotes

[2]Ladislaus Boros, *We Are Future* (New York: Herder and Herder, 1970), 133-134.

[3]Haughey, *Conspiracy of God*, p. 94.

Chapter 18B

[1]Nouwen, *The Wounded Healer*, pp. 86-87.

[2]Johannes B. Metz, *Poverty of Spirit* (New York: Newman, 1968), 39-40.

[3]Anne Philipe, *Le Temps d'un Soupir*, (Paris: R. Juilliard, 1963), 49.

Chapter 18C

[1]James L. Connor, S.J., "Jesuit Community," in Supplement to *The Way*, No. 19, Summer, 1973, 84.

Chapter 19

[1]Maurice Bellet, *La Peur ou la Foi* (Paris-Bruges: Desclée De Brouwer, 1967), 177.

Chapter 21

[1]Edward Farrell, *Surprised by the Spirit* (Denville, N.J.: Dimension Books, 1973), 105.